READ THE PASSAGE Think about what a real dog can do.

Sparky the Wonder Dog

Bella's dog Sparky likes to run and explore. Bella thinks that Sparky is like a magician. One moment Sparky is in the backyard and then, all of a sudden, he's gone!

Sparky escaped again last week, so Bella set out to find him. She called out Sparky's name as she walked. Bella even shook Sparky's bag of dog chow. "Treats! Treats!" yelled Bella. Sparky loved his treats, but he did not appear.

Then Bella stopped. She smelled some meat grilling. She spotted a cloud of smoke from behind a house. Bella headed there and peeked in the yard. Sure enough, there was Sparky. He stood on his hind legs in front of a grill. Sparky was whistling and flipping burgers. Bella could see Sparky's mouth drool. Bella wondered where Sparky got the apron he was wearing.

STRATEGY PRACTICE Circle the word or words and complete the sentence.

I (would   would not) like to have Sparky as a pet because _____

_____.

SKILL PRACTICE Read the item. Write your response.

1. Did this story really happen? How do you know?

_____

2. Why was drool coming from Sparky's mouth?

_____

3. After Bella found Sparky, do you think he rushed to get the dog chow she had? Tell why or why not.

_____

READ THE PASSAGE Think about a time when you learned something new.

Whoa, Boy!

Evan lived in the city. More than anything, he wanted to ride a horse. He could hardly wait to gallop as fast as the wind. Evan visited Uncle Pete at his farm. His uncle was ready to show Evan how to ride.

Evan sat on a fence as his uncle walked a horse toward him. The ground seemed to shake with every step the horse took. Evan dug his fingernails into the fence. He stared at the huge beast. "Were all horses this big?" he wondered.

Uncle Pete helped Evan onto the horse's back. Then Evan tapped the horse's sides with his heels. The horse began to trot. Evan bounced up and down like a jumping frog.

"Riding a horse hurts," said Evan. He decided to forget about galloping. For now, the speed of a merry-go-round seemed just right.

STRATEGY PRACTICE Circle the word or words and complete the sentence.

When I learned something new, I (felt   did not feel) like Evan because _____

_____.

SKILL PRACTICE Read the item. Write your response.

1. How did Evan feel before he arrived at the farm? Which sentence lets you know?

_____

_____

2. Why did Evan dig his fingernails into the fence when he saw the horse?

_____

3. Did Evan enjoy his ride? How do you know?

_____

READ THE PASSAGE Look for how chimpanzees' behavior is like human behavior.

Learning About Chimpanzees

We know a lot about chimpanzees because of Jane Goodall. She studied the apes for over 30 years. She crawled through thick forests in Africa to sit still and watch them. During that time, Jane wrote down what she saw and heard.

We now know that chimpanzees live in friendly groups. They greet each other with a hug and a kiss. Mother chimps tickle their babies and make them laugh. Chimpanzees play games together, and they clean each other. They show their feelings, too. Worried chimpanzees pucker their lips. Scared chimpanzees bare their teeth. Calm and happy chimpanzees smile. And each sound a chimpanzee makes means something. For example, chimpanzees bark when they find food.

Chimpanzees also solve problems. They use sticks as tools to get food they cannot reach. They chew leaves and use them as sponges to sop up water.

STRATEGY PRACTICE Complete the sentence.

I was surprised to read that chimpanzees _____.

SKILL PRACTICE Read the item. Write your response.

1. Why was Jane Goodall able to learn so much about chimpanzees?

_____

2. Where do chimpanzees live? How do you know?

_____

_____

3. Name three ways in which chimpanzees act like humans.

_____

_____

READ THE PASSAGE   Think about what makes people grouchy or grumpy.

Charles the Grouch

Charles did not care to smile, but he did like to complain. When the day was sunny, Charles said it was too hot. When the birds sang, he said they were too loud. Charles said parties were too crowded and rainbows were too colorful.

One day, Charles was in his garden grumbling that the carrots were too orange. And he thought the trees were too tall. Suddenly, an elf appeared. The elf spoke slowly, as he tried to control his anger. The elf said, "I have heard enough of your complaining. You grumble all day. You fuss all night. I am going to grant you three wishes. Then perhaps you will stop being such a grouch!"

"Only three wishes? Why can't I have more than three?" whined Charles.

"Forget it! No wishes for you!" yelled the elf. The elf disappeared.

"They were probably crummy wishes anyway," Charles complained.

STRATEGY PRACTICE   Answer the question.

How do you act around grumpy people? _____

_____

SKILL PRACTICE   Read the item. Write your response.

1. If you met Charles, what expression would you expect to see on his face? Why?

_____

_____

2. Why do you think Charles was always complaining?

_____

3. If you were the elf, would you have disappeared? Explain.

_____

READ THE PASSAGE Think about the colors of birds you have seen.

Odd Baby Birds

Waxwings are small songbirds. They have pale yellow bellies and yellow tips on their tail feathers. Some young waxwings are odd because they look different from their parents. Those young birds have tail feathers with orange tips. Scientists have discovered why. The answer has to do with food.

Waxwings mostly eat berries. One kind of honeysuckle plant grows in some places. The plant's berries grow for just a short time. The berries have a strong red color. Some waxwings feed a lot of those red berries to their babies. Their babies might be growing tail feathers at that time. If they are, the red color settles in their tail feathers. Instead of having yellow tips like their parents, their feathers are tipped in orange.

STRATEGY PRACTICE Tell a partner about the strangest bird you have ever seen.

SKILL PRACTICE Read the item. Write your response.

1. Name three ways in which waxwings are similar to other birds.

_____

_____

2. What would happen if a baby bird did not eat red berries while growing its tail feathers?

_____

_____

3. Compare the appearance of your favorite bird with the adult waxwing.

_____

_____

READ THE PASSAGE   Visualize a dog doing each action described in the passage.

Ways Dogs Talk

Dogs use their voices and bodies to talk to people. Watch a dog's actions. You can learn to tell what it is trying to say.

A dog shows when it is happy to see you. It looks at you and wags its tail, or it runs around quickly in circles. Some happy dogs will jump up on you. A scared dog acts differently than a happy dog. A frightened dog puts its tail down between its legs. Some scared dogs growl. Others try to hide.

Dogs like being with people, so they try to get your attention. They tap you with a paw or place their head in your lap. They also might look at you and bark or howl.

Dogs show when they want to be left alone, too. A dog that is upset will bare its teeth, or it will growl. Both are signs to stay away!

STRATEGY PRACTICE   Think back to the dog's actions you pictured while you read. With a partner, describe a dog doing two of those actions.

SKILL PRACTICE   Read the item. Write your response.

1. What are two reasons that a dog might growl?

_____

_____

2. Picture an unfamiliar dog running toward you with a wagging tail. What can you assume?

_____

_____

3. You see your friend's dog hiding behind a chair. Should you try to touch it? Explain.

_____

_____

READ THE PASSAGE Visualize Fabio's first two days at camp.

No Camp for Me!

Fabio was new at summer camp, and he did not like it at all. In fact, he hated every minute of it.

On his first day, he and the other campers swam in a lake. The bottom of the lake felt like muddy slime creeping between Fabio's toes. He dashed out of the water when a fish nibbled at his knee.

Fabio's second day started badly. The campers hiked through some woods. Dry twigs scratched Fabio's legs, and black bugs bit his arms. The stinky smell of a skunk made his eyes water. Fabio walked behind the others. He wished he were at home. Then a boy named Cody started talking to Fabio. It turned out that they liked playing the same games. They made a deal to try out for the camp softball team. Fabio thought the next day at camp would be fun.

STRATEGY PRACTICE Look back at the story. Circle four describing words that helped you picture Fabio at camp.

SKILL PRACTICE Read the item. Write your response.

1. Picture the lake that Fabio swam in. Describe what it looks like.

_____

_____

2. Imagine Fabio and Cody on the third day of camp. What are they doing?

_____

_____

3. Which of Fabio's bad camp experiences was the worst? Why?

_____

_____

READ THE PASSAGE Visualize what is the same and what is different about the two seabirds.

Puffins and Penguins

Penguins and puffins are two kinds of seabirds. They both are black and white. And they both have webbed feet. However, puffins are much smaller than penguins. Puffins are more colorful, too. Puffins have bright orange beaks, legs, and feet. Penguins have black beaks, and their feet are often black, too.

You won't find puffins and penguins living together. Penguins live far south, and puffins live far north. But they both depend on the sea for their food. Both birds have sharp spikes in their mouths. The spikes hold on to the fish they catch.

Although penguins and puffins are birds, penguins cannot fly. Their wings are too stiff. Penguins' wings, however, work as flippers. They allow penguins to dive deep into the sea. Puffins use their wings for flying and for diving. But they cannot dive as deep as penguins.

STRATEGY PRACTICE Draw and then color a puffin's feet and a penguin's feet.

SKILL PRACTICE Read the item. Write your response.

1. Which bird eats larger fish? How do you know?

_____

_____

2. Which bird can you picture soaring above the ocean? Why?

_____

_____

3. What can a penguin do with its wings?

_____

_____

READ THE PASSAGE Visualize the work the kids do.

Puffin Patrol

The flashlight's beam lights up a frightened face. Small hands grab the fuzzy creature. Then it is stowed in a box. Children work through the night to capture baby puffins. The kids are part of the Puffin Patrol.

The kids live on an island off the coast of Iceland. In the spring, puffins roost on the island's cliffs. Each female lays one egg. By the middle of August, the baby seabirds are ready to leave their nests. They know to head toward the ocean. Lights from the night sky reflect on the sea. Most of the birds go toward those lights. But some babies fly toward the lights of the town. They crash-land in yards, parking lots, and streets.

Cats, dogs, and cars might harm the baby birds. So kids gather them up. In the morning, they carry their boxes of puffins to the sea. The kids toss the birds high into the air. The young seabirds glide on the wind and then land on the water. They are safe at home.

STRATEGY PRACTICE With a partner, act out the finding and saving of baby puffins.

SKILL PRACTICE Read the item. Write your response.

1. Reread the first sentence. Explain whose face is frightened and why.

_____

_____

2. Picture the baby puffins as they hatch. Describe where they are.

_____

_____

3. Why is there a Puffin Patrol on the island?

_____

_____

READ THE PASSAGE Visualize each animal as it enters the mitten.

Achooooo!

One cold day, a squirrel saw a mitten lying on the snow. The squirrel crawled inside where it was warm and cozy. Soon after, a rabbit joined the squirrel. The two animals fit just right until a skunk peeked in. Not wanting to anger the skunk, the rabbit invited it to stay. A fox then followed the skunk. All of the animals were very snug indeed. Before long, a bear came by. The bear insisted on using the mitten for his long winter nap. The bear squeezed in and a mouse did, too. It sat on the only space left—the top of the bear's nose. The mouse's tail swished back and forth, back and forth. The bear sneezed like a roll of thunder. Out flew the animals! Never again did they try to turn a mitten into a home.

STRATEGY PRACTICE Draw the mitten <u>before</u> the squirrel crawls in. Then draw the mitten <u>after</u> the bear enters it.

SKILL PRACTICE Read the item. Write your response.

1. Why did the animals move into the mitten?

_____

2. What caused the bear to sneeze?

_____

3. Could this story happen? How do you know?

_____

_____

Daily Reading Comprehension • EMC 6363 • © Evan-Moor Corp.

READ THE PASSAGE Notice words that help you understand when things happen.

Ready, Aim, Spit!

An archerfish can get its food in two ways. It can leap out of the water to snag a bug. Or it can stay in the water and shoot down its food by spitting a jet of water.

The fish begins the attack by first swimming near a low branch. It stays underwater but close to the surface. Only the tip of its mouth sticks out of the water. Next, the fish waits for a bug to land on the branch. When the bug lands, the archerfish acts quickly. First, the fish presses its tongue against a groove on the roof of its mouth. This makes a narrow tube. Then, it snaps its gills shut. This action forces water into its mouth and out the tube. Zap! The jet of water hits the bug, which falls into the water. With a gulp, the archerfish finally eats its meal.

STRATEGY PRACTICE Circle the signal words that helped you understand how the passage was organized.

SKILL PRACTICE Read the item. Write your response.

1. When an archerfish is hungry, where does it go?

_____

_____

2. Why does the archerfish press its tongue against the roof of its mouth?

_____

_____

3. What happens if the archerfish misses the bug?

_____

_____

READ THE PASSAGE Notice how the author feels about earthworms.

Wiggly Workers

Some people think earthworms are yucky. I think earthworms are a farmer's best friend.

To grow healthy plants, a farmer needs healthy soil. Earthworms help make soil healthy and rich. These wiggly critters live in the ground where it is moist and cool. They move by digging tunnels. Each time earthworms wiggle, they mix and sift the soil. This loosens the dirt so that plants can spread their roots. The worms' digging actions also bring air into the soil, which plants need to live. Earthworms eat tiny bits of plants and dead bugs. The droppings that earthworms deposit are nutrients. They make the soil rich for growing fruits and vegetables.

I think farmers will agree with me. Earthworms are amazing creatures!

STRATEGY PRACTICE Underline two sentences that tell why earthworms are good for farmers.

SKILL PRACTICE Read the item. Write your response.

1. How would crops do if planted in a field with very few earthworms? Why?

_____

_____

2. What do gardeners probably think about earthworms? Explain.

_____

_____

3. Name three ways in which earthworms affect the soil.

_____

_____

READ THE PASSAGE Think about reasons why travel to the West was uncomfortable.

Rugged Roads

In the 1800s, people moved to the West in covered wagons. Mules or oxen pulled the wagons. Families piled their furniture and belongings inside. Because the wagons were so full, there was no room in the wagon for sleeping.

Traveling was an adventure. The wagons were not comfortable to ride in because the wagon wheels were covered in iron, not rubber. Roads made wagons more uncomfortable because they were bumpy and not paved. People who did not drive the wagon walked beside it.

The roads were rugged, but they did help with one daily chore. Women or children milked their cows in the morning. Then they poured some fresh milk into a wooden butter churn. They hung the container on the wagon. The wagon bounced so much that by night, the churn held a lump of butter.

STRATEGY PRACTICE Look back at the second paragraph. Write a *C* above each <u>cause</u>. Write an *E* above each <u>effect</u>.

SKILL PRACTICE Read the item. Write your response.

1. What was the effect of the unpaved roads?

_____

_____

2. Why did people walk beside the wagons rather than ride in them?

_____

_____

3. Why didn't families sleep in their covered wagons?

_____

_____

READ THE PASSAGE   Look for words that tell you how each paragraph is organized.

Rub That Mud!

Baseball teams use a lot of new balls in every game. Each team must have at least 90 on hand. The balls are white and shiny when they get to the park. But they are not shiny when the game begins. This is because shiny balls are slippery to throw. Pitchers might hurt the batters with wild pitches. So each ball is rubbed with a special mud. The mud makes the balls safer to use.

All the baseball teams use the same mud. It is made and sold by one company. First, a crew goes to a secret location. Next, they dig up hundreds of pounds of muck. Then, they rinse the mud to get rid of rocks. Some secret ingredients are added. They make the mud feel like creamy pudding. Finally, the mud is stored in barrels.

After six to eight weeks, the mud is ready to send to the ballparks. One worker at each park takes care of the new balls. The worker adds water to a dab of mud and rubs it onto each ball. About an hour later, over 100 balls are ready for play.

STRATEGY PRACTICE   Look back at the second paragraph and underline the words that signal the order of steps.

SKILL PRACTICE   Read the item. Write your response.

1. What happens after the mud is rinsed?

_____

_____

2. What sentence in the text tells you why all the teams use the same mud?

_____

3. Who does the final step in getting the shine off the baseballs?

_____

_____

READ THE PASSAGE Think about the main idea and details in each paragraph.

Is She Smarter Than a Fifth-Grader?

Grace is no ordinary four-year-old. Grace dunks basketballs and plays the piano. And she's an artist, too. Grace holds a brush between her big front teeth and paints pictures. People buy her paintings, and the money is given to the poor. Yes, Grace is very clever, especially for a mule.

Mules usually do as they please. But that's not Grace. Steve Foster, her owner, says that Grace is a fast learner. She uses the different sounds of his voice to know and follow his commands. Grace may be the smartest mule in the world! Being smart helped her get a part in a movie. She appears in the film *Get Low* and plays a mule, of course. Because Grace plays an old mule, she wears makeup. Her face has white and gray coloring.

STRATEGY PRACTICE Underline two sentences in the first paragraph that tell you things that Grace does that make her clever.

SKILL PRACTICE Read the item. Write your response.

1. Why did the author wait until the end of the first paragraph to say that Grace is a mule?

_____

_____

2. Write three details that tell how Grace differs from other mules.

_____

_____

3. What did Grace have to do for her movie role?

_____

_____

READ THE PASSAGE   Think about the information that is most important.

How to Groom a Zooraffa

If you're thinking about getting a pet zooraffa, there is something you should know. Grooming a zooraffa takes work. Here are the steps to follow:

1. Make an appointment at a carwash on a rainy day.
2. Loosen the dirt on your zooraffa. A garden rake works best. Pull the rake through the fur about 50 times. Wear a mask to keep the dirt out of your eyes.
3. Get a big blanket and some bubble bath. The bubble bath can smell nice, like vanilla or sweet potatoes.
4. Put a strong leash on your pet and walk it to the carwash. Stay away from busy streets.
5. Squirt some bubble bath on your zooraffa and send it through the wash.
6. Afterward, use the blanket to clean between the zooraffa's toes.
7. Reward your zooraffa for getting clean. Toss it a porcupine pie.

STRATEGY PRACTICE   With a partner, retell the steps for grooming a zooraffa. Use only the most important information.

SKILL PRACTICE   Read the item. Write your response.

1. Why did the author use numbering in this text?

_____

2. What conclusion can you draw about the size of a zooraffa? Why?

_____

_____

3. What should the owner do after arriving at the carwash?

_____

_____

READ THE PASSAGE Think about what the author wants you to know.
How does the author give you this information?

Garcia Earns Trophy

On Saturday afternoon, four boys took part in the finals of the high jump. The exciting event took place at Breakers Stadium. Fans filled the stands to cheer for the boys. Each boy was allowed three jumps. All three jumps were averaged to decide the final scores. All four boys were good athletes. But Frankie Garcia's skills topped the others'. He won the first-place trophy.

Athletes	Scores
Garcia	5 feet (1.5 m)
Rashad	4 feet 8 inches (1.4 m)
Brenner	4 feet 6 inches (1.3 m)
Welsh	3 feet 7 inches (1.1 m)

STRATEGY PRACTICE Circle two sentences in the passage that have the most important information about who won the high-jump event.

SKILL PRACTICE Read the item. Write your response.

1. How were the final scores determined?

_____

_____

2. What important information appears in the text but not in the picture?

_____

_____

3. Where can the reader find Brenner's final score? What was it?

_____

READ THE PASSAGE Remember the most important facts about boas.

Boas are large, powerful snakes. Some types of boas are as long as 18 feet (5.5 m). All boas have strong muscles that help them move and help them eat.

Where Boas Live

Boas are found mostly in forests in parts of Mexico and South America. They live on the ground, in trees, and in or near water. Boas are good swimmers. They also can climb trees, twist around branches, and hang by their tails. Their body colors and skin patterns blend into the trees.

How Boas Eat

Boas are meat eaters. They hunt at night for small animals and birds. They first grab their prey with their teeth. Then they squeeze their prey to kill it. They swallow their food whole and do not chew.

STRATEGY PRACTICE Underline three sentences that tell more about where a boa lives and what a boa eats.

SKILL PRACTICE Read the item. Write your response.

1. Where in the text would a reader look for information about boas' prey?

_____

_____

2. What does a boa do after grabbing prey with its teeth?

_____

_____

3. What would be a good title for this text?

_____

_____

READ THE PASSAGE Think about the information that is most important for making peanut butter.

The Food That Goes with Jelly

Making peanut butter is a big business. Peanuts grow underground. Around 40 peanuts grow on one plant. Special tractors dig up the plants and lay them upside down on the ground. The peanuts stay in the sun until they are dry. Next, stems and rocks are removed. After the peanuts are cleaned, they are shelled and roasted. Then, they are cooled. The cooled peanuts are rubbed gently to remove their skins. Finally, the peanuts are ground into a paste. Sometimes, sugar, salt, and oil are added.

Groundnut crop calendar for most of the United States											
			Plant					**Harvest**			
Jan	Feb	Mar	Apr	May	Jun	Jul	Aug	Sept	Oct	Nov	Dec

STRATEGY PRACTICE In the passage, underline three sentences that are important in telling the steps to make peanut butter.

SKILL PRACTICE Read the item. Write your response.

1. Why are peanuts left in the field for a while?

_____

_____

2. What ingredients besides peanuts may be in peanut butter?

_____

3. In the United States, when are peanuts removed from the ground? How do you know?

_____

_____

READ THE PAGE   Think about the kind of information that is given in a dictionary.

bat

bat (bat) **1.** A wooden stick or club used to hit a ball. **2.** A flying mammal with wings of thin skin. noun

blimp (blimp) A kind of balloon that can be steered: *A blimp is filled with a gas that is lighter than air.* See picture. noun

blizzard (bliz′ erd) A very cold snowstorm with strong winds: *The blizzard covered our house with snow.* noun

boil (boil) To bubble up and give off steam: *The hot water began to boil.* verb

broken (bro′ ken) In pieces: *The cup was broken.* adjective

STRATEGY PRACTICE   Which information in a dictionary is the most important? Why?

_____

SKILL PRACTICE   Read the item. Write your response.

1. Look at the entry for *blizzard*. What does it tell you besides the definition?

_____

_____

2. Why does the word *bat* come before the word *blizzard* on the page?

_____

_____

3. Why did the dictionary show a picture of a blimp?

_____

READ THE PASSAGE Think about what you want to know about living in Japan.

Fumi's House

Kara likes getting e-mail from Fumi. Kara is a third-grader in Arizona, and Fumi is in third grade in Japan. They are e-pals who send e-mails every week. Fumi sent Kara photos and descriptions of her home.

The first room in Fumi's house is a small entryway. People who enter the home remove their shoes. They put on different shoes with soft soles. That seemed odd to Kara. She wears her street shoes in the house.

Kara likes the photo of Fumi and her family eating. They gather around a table, just like Kara and her family. Kara's family sits on chairs, but Fumi's family sits on cushions on a straw mat on the floor. The table is low to the ground. What seems to be a wall behind Fumi's family is actually a door without knobs. Fumi explained that the door slides open. It is made from strong paper glued to thin strips of wood. "I could never play ball in that house!" thought Kara.

STRATEGY PRACTICE Write a question you have about the passage.

_____

SKILL PRACTICE Read the item. Write your response.

1. What are doors like inside Japanese homes?

_____

_____

2. How are Fumi's and Kara's lives similar?

_____

_____

3. When Kara and Fumi enter their own homes, what do they do differently?

_____

READ THE PASSAGE   After each paragraph, think of a question you have.

The Paper in Paper Money

You can fold paper money and write on it and draw on it, too. Paper money seems to be like the notebook paper you use in school. But it's not the same.

Notebook paper, like most other kinds of paper, is made of wood fibers from trees. Fibers are parts of wood that are shaped like long, thin threads. Paper money is made from cotton and linen plants. They are pounded together to form strong fibers. Those fibers hold together firmly. So, money is stronger than notebook paper.

People use linen and cotton paper to make money so that it will last longer. This way, people don't have to make a lot of new money all the time. Also, it is harder for someone to make fake money because it is hard to find paper made from linen and cotton. In fact, the company that makes the paper for our money doesn't make paper for anyone else!

STRATEGY PRACTICE   Write one question you asked while reading the passage.

_____

SKILL PRACTICE   Read the item. Write your response.

1. Which is stronger: notebook paper or paper money? Why?

_____

_____

2. What was the author's purpose for writing this text?

_____

_____

3. Can anyone buy paper made of linen and cotton? How do you know?

_____

READ THE PASSAGE Think of questions that can be answered with information from the passage.

A Clever Spinner

The spider laughed with excitement. She was ready to build her very first web. The place between the tree branches was perfect. So the spider did exactly as her mother had shown her.

The spider pulled a thread of silk from her body. She tugged hard to make it strong. Then she focused on her work. Back and forth, up and down, and around and around the spider dashed. She transformed her silk into an orb web with a spiral center.

Feeling very pleased, the spider did not stop. She began to try other shapes. By nightfall, she had spun webs that looked like the Statue of Liberty and the Empire State Building. "Bugs on vacation will want to visit these," she chuckled.

STRATEGY PRACTICE Write a question about the passage. Have a partner answer it.

_____

SKILL PRACTICE Read the item. Write your response.

1. What parts of this text could actually happen?

_____

_____

2. What does the word *transformed* mean? How do you know?

_____

_____

3. How did the author combine information with entertainment in this text?

_____

_____

READ THE PASSAGE Ask yourself what is the same and what is different about the Arctic and Antarctica.

Earth's Top and Bottom

Earth's top and bottom are more different than alike. The Arctic is the farthest place north. It is an icy ocean surrounded by land. Antarctica is the farthest place south. It is a frozen land surrounded by ocean. Both places are too cold to rain. Very little snow falls in either place because the air is as dry as a desert.

Large areas of land surround the Arctic Ocean. The land closest to the Arctic is always frozen deep down into the soil. But in the summer, the weather is mild. Some plants grow then, and wolves, foxes, and birds feed on them.

Unlike the Arctic, all of Antarctica is covered in ice that never melts. It is the coldest place on Earth. Only tiny insects live there. But sea animals live in the icy ocean around Antarctica. Emperor penguins live on ice packs near the coast.

STRATEGY PRACTICE Write a question about the passage. Have a partner answer it.

_____

SKILL PRACTICE Read the item. Write your response.

1. Name three ways in which the Arctic and Antarctica are alike.

_____

_____

2. Name three ways in which the Arctic and Antarctica are different.

_____

_____

3. Write one question you have about the Arctic or Antarctica.

_____

_____

READ THE PASSAGE As you read, think of questions that help you imagine the characters and setting in the passage.

Follow Our Light

Fireflies sparked in the night sky. Zack grabbed a few and put them into a jar. He would bring them to show-and-tell tomorrow. He looked at the bugs in the jar. The fireflies flew in slow circles. Their quick flickers of light sparkled like stars.

Zack started walking home. He lived outside of town. There were no neighborhoods or streetlights. Zack was finding his way home without a problem until a cloud slid in front of the moon. That's when he wished he had his flashlight. Zack's stomach flip-flopped as he tried to find his way in the dark.

Zack heard tiny voices. The fireflies were calling to him! "Let us out and we will show you the way home," one firefly said. Zack opened the jar, and the fireflies flew out. They danced in the air in front of Zack. Their light turned the night into day. Zack's stomach settled down. Soon, he was back home. Zack thanked the fireflies. They flashed brightly before flying off into the night.

STRATEGY PRACTICE Write a question that helped you pay closer attention to the passage or helped you enjoy it more.

_____

SKILL PRACTICE Read the item. Write your response.

1. Is this a fantasy? How do you know?

_____

2. How do you think the fireflies felt about being in Zack's jar? Why?

_____

_____

3. Did the author write this story to teach readers about fireflies? Explain.

_____

READ THE TABLE OF CONTENTS   As you read, think about how you would use a table of contents.

This table of contents is in a book about the country of Italy.

Table of Contents

STRATEGY PRACTICE   Write one way that reading a table of contents is different from reading a story.

_____

SKILL PRACTICE   Read the item. Write your response.

1. When would you use a table of contents?

_____

_____

2. On what page does chapter 3 begin? How do you know?

_____

_____

3. Which chapter would have information on Italy in World War II? Why?

_____

Pay attention to how Nathan feels throughout the passage.

Birthday Blues

Nathan woke up early and raced into the kitchen. He saw his family eating cereal and toast just like every other day. Where were his birthday presents? Where was his birthday cake? Did his family forget his special day?

The doorbell rang. Nathan opened the door, but no one was there. All he saw was a note on the ground. The note said that Nathan was going on a treasure hunt, and he would need to find the clues. The first clue was in the desert. Nathan was confused. Then he smiled and headed to his sister's sandbox. There was the second clue. Nathan spent an hour following one clue after another. Finally, he got to the last note. All it said was *Happy Birthday*. There was no treasure!

Nathan wiped away his tears. He slowly walked back to his house with his head hung low. He couldn't see the balloons inside the house. He did not see the people quickly hiding.

STRATEGY PRACTICE Tell a partner what you visualized after you read the first paragraph and how you checked your mental image.

SKILL PRACTICE Read the item. Write your response.

1. What was Nathan's family doing inside the house while he followed the clues?

_____

2. How does Nathan feel after finding the last clue? Which sentences in the text show this?

_____

_____

3. What will happen next?

_____

_____

READ THE PASSAGE   As you read, underline the words you do not know or the parts you do not understand.

An Aquatic Mystery

An aquarium is a building with a lot of water in a lot of tanks. People go there to see the aquatic animals and plants that live in the tanks.

One morning, workers arrived at an aquarium in California. They were ready for work. They were not ready to mop. But that's what they had to do. Water was all over the floor outside the shark tank and the ray tank. Water squished under the workers' shoes as they walked. There were no leaks or broken tanks. What caused the flood?

The troublemaker turned out to be an eight-armed creature. The small octopus lived in its own tank. It weighed only one pound (.5 kg). But it was curious and quite active, too. During the night, the octopus crawled to the top of its tank. It pulled out a tube that was bringing in water. The tube sprayed seawater outside of the tank. The water flowed for almost 10 hours. About 200 gallons (750 L) spilled onto the aquarium floor. That's a big mess for a one-pound octopus!

STRATEGY PRACTICE   Ask questions about the words in the passage you do not know or the parts you do not understand.

SKILL PRACTICE   Read the item. Write your response.

1. What other animals are housed near the octopus? How do you know?

_____

2. What would have happened if the octopus did this when the aquarium was open?

_____

_____

3. Picture what happened. How can the aquarium keep this from happening again?

_____

READ THE PASSAGE Stop after each section and tell yourself the important ideas.

A Tricky Creature

An octopus tricks its enemies in different ways.

You Can't See Me!

An octopus can hide without going anywhere. It changes the way it looks so that it can't be seen. An octopus can change the color, pattern, or texture of its skin. An octopus can look like a rock or like sand. It can turn red, orange, brown, black, white, or gray.

Away I Go!

When in danger, an octopus can squirt a cloud of ink. The ink confuses the animal that is attacking the octopus. To get away fast, the octopus takes in water. Then it forces the water out of an opening in its body. Away jets the octopus!

An octopus can use rocks as an escape route, too. It squeezes its soft body into the small spaces between rocks. No shark, dolphin, or eel can follow it there.

STRATEGY PRACTICE Did your mind wander as you read? What did you do to focus on what you were reading?

SKILL PRACTICE Read the item. Write your response.

1. Picture an octopus in open water. A predator swims close. What does the octopus do?

_____

_____

2. What predators want to eat an octopus? How do you know?

_____

_____

3. How can an octopus hide without moving?

_____

READ THE PASSAGE   As you read, pay close attention to the facts.

A New Invention

The first drinking straws grew outdoors. People broke off a piece of hollow grass. They plunked it into their cold lemonade and then sipped. Holding a glass with warm hands warmed the drink. So the grass helped keep the lemonade cold. But, ripe grass also changed how the lemonade tasted.

Marvin Stone wanted something that worked better than grass. He liked working with paper. So, he wrapped a strip of paper around a pencil. He glued the edges closed. Sure enough, his paper drinking straw worked. He then tried thicker paper that he covered in a thin wax. That paper did not fall apart in a drink.

Mr. Stone experimented with different sizes of straws. He decided that $8\frac{1}{2}$ inches (22 cm) was the perfect length for a straw. He found the best width, too. It let the drink through but kept lemon seeds out.

STRATEGY PRACTICE   Tell a partner one way to stay focused while reading.

SKILL PRACTICE   Read the item. Write your response.

1. Who invented the drinking straw and why?

_____

_____

2. Why were paper straws coated with thin wax?

_____

_____

3. How did the inventor choose the ideal width of a straw?

_____

_____

READ THE PASSAGE Think about the main idea and important details in each paragraph.

Seashells Are Their Homes

Seashells are the empty homes of some sea animals. Those animals need shells to protect their soft bodies. They have no bones.

Some sea animals live inside a shell. Sea snails live inside a shell that is usually twisted or curved. The shell covers the sea snail's body. But its head and foot stick out from the shell when the snail moves. The sea snail pulls its head and foot inside when it needs to hide.

Other sea animals live inside a shell that has two parts that connect. A clam, for example, lives inside two shells. The shells connect along one side. The clam is safe inside. Clams use their strong muscles to open and close their shells to get food.

SKILL PRACTICE Read the item. Write your response.

1. Which sentence states the overall main idea of the text?

_____

_____

2. When in danger, how does a sea snail protect itself?

_____

_____

3. What is the main idea of the third paragraph?

_____

_____

STRATEGY PRACTICE Tell a partner three things that you learned about sea animals.

READ THE PASSAGE   Look for sentences that give the most important ideas.

A Small School

Would you want to go to school in a national park? What if the park was the hottest and driest place in the country? What if it was called Death Valley? Death Valley National Park is a beautiful but harsh desert. For five months a year, temperatures soar over 100°F (38°C).

About 500 people live in Death Valley, and some work in the park. Many of the people are families with young children. Death Valley Elementary School is down the road from the visitors' center. The school is located on Old Ghost Road. In spite of the scary name, the school is a happy place. The building has two rooms, and it had 11 students in 2009. Most of the students are kindergartners, and the oldest student is in 4th grade. One teacher and one aide work with all of the students. Going to school in a place called Death Valley can be a good thing. In such a small school, each student gets a lot of attention.

SKILL PRACTICE   Read the item. Write your response.

1. What is the second paragraph mainly about?

_____

_____

2. What makes Death Valley National Park so unusual?

_____

_____

3. Which detail supports the idea that the school is a happy place?

_____

_____

STRATEGY PRACTICE   Tell a partner three important details about Death Valley.

Daily Reading Comprehension • EMC 6363 • © Evan-Moor Corp.

READ THE PASSAGE Remember the important steps in making the candy.

Making a Sweet Treat

Mix, color, and shine. Those are a few of the steps it takes to make candy corn. Huge machines do all of the work.

Machines first mix together honey, sugar, salt, and other ingredients. They are mixed until they form batches of soft candy. The soft candy is divided into three parts. Then each part is dyed white, yellow, or orange. Each color of candy is placed inside its own machine. It flows out of the machine and lands inside molds, or forms. Each mold is the size and shape of one candy corn. The white color goes into the top of the mold. The orange candy pours into the middle, and the yellow flows into the bottom.

After the candy dries, it is covered with cooking oil and wax. Then the candy is ready for the final step. The candy corn pieces are placed inside machines that spin. The pieces rub gently against each other until they shine.

SKILL PRACTICE Read the item. Write your response.

1. What steps must be done before the candy is poured into molds?

_____

_____

2. In what order do the colors go into the molds?

_____

_____

3. What is the final step? How does it affect the candy corn?

_____

STRATEGY PRACTICE Look back at the passage and number the first three steps in making candy corn.

READ THE PASSAGE Think about the most important steps in making a stamp.

Stamping Made Easy

Stamping is a fun way to decorate paper. You can buy rubber stamps and ink pads in craft stores. Or you can make your own stamps by following these steps:

1. Cover a table with newspaper.
2. Get your supplies: pieces of cardboard, scissors, glue, ink pad, and paper.
3. Cut a piece of the cardboard into a square. Cut a shape out of another piece of cardboard.
4. Glue the shape onto the square. Let the glue dry. Now you have a stamp.
5. Press the stamp onto the ink pad.
6. Press the stamp firmly onto the paper.
7. Make a print of the shape over and over again. Put the ink on the stamp each time you print.

Now that you have the idea, you can get fancy. Use more than one shape. Show your prints to a friend.

SKILL PRACTICE Read the item. Write your response.

1. Why is the first step covering the table with newspaper?

_____

_____

2. What can you do as soon as the glue is dry?

_____

_____

3. Would it be more fun to buy stamps or make your own? Explain.

_____

STRATEGY PRACTICE Make a numbered list of instructions for an activity you like to do.

Daily Reading Comprehension • EMC 6363 • © Evan-Moor Corp.

Notice the order of events.

Liam Baby-sits

Gus and Bret started crying as soon as their mother closed the door. They didn't want her to leave. Liam, their baby sitter, tried to distract the boys. "Let's play hide-and-seek. You guys hide and I'll count to ten. Then I'll try to find you." Liam found Gus under a chair and Bret behind a door. They played over and over again. Each time, the two boys hid in the same places. Finally, Liam could not stand to play one more time. "Let's take the dog for a walk," he said.

Big Bertha pulled her leash and Liam, too. Gus ran one way and Bret dashed the other. Liam had to act fast. He decided to bribe the boys into behaving. "Whoever walks back to the house with me can have a snack!" Liam shouted.

At home, the boys chomped on some cookies and got ready for a nap. They demanded a story. Liam told them the story of the little red hen over and over again. When Mrs. Hobbs returned home, she found three sleeping boys.

SKILL PRACTICE Read the item. Write your response.

1. About how old are Gus and Bret?

_____

_____

2. When did Liam bribe the boys? Why did he do it?

_____

_____

3. What do the boys do just before the story of the little red hen?

_____

STRATEGY PRACTICE Tell a partner three things Liam did with the boys in the order that he did them.

READ THE PASSAGE   Look for how a volcano causes an island to form.

How an Island Is Formed

Most islands are located in oceans. Many of these islands are the tops of huge volcanoes. The volcanoes go all the way down to the bottom of the sea. But they began *under* the ocean floor. The ocean floor is part of a layer of Earth called the **crust**. It is very hot underneath the crust, so the rocks there are soft. Those hot, soft rocks rise through cracks in Earth's crust. That action is the beginning of an underwater volcano.

When hot rocks rise through the crust, they hit the water. The water cools the rocks and hardens them. As more hot rocks spill out of the cracks, layers of rocks build up. Over a long period of time, the layers can get higher and higher. As a result, the underwater volcano might rise out of the ocean. The top of that volcano is an island.

SKILL PRACTICE   Read the item. Write your response.

1. What are rocks like under the ocean's floor?

_____

_____

2. How does water affect hot rocks?

_____

_____

3. What happens when underwater volcanoes reach the sea's surface?

_____

_____

STRATEGY PRACTICE   Underline words and phrases in the passage that helped you visualize how an island is formed.

READ THE PASSAGE Think about the reasons why Mia acts the way she does in the passage.

Mia in the Kitchen

Mia's elbows were leaned on the kitchen table. She sat with her chin in her hands and her eyes looking down. A plate of cookies was in front of her. Like all third-graders, Mia liked summer vacation. But when there was nothing to do, she got bored.

As Mia munched on a cookie, she knew just what to do. She would bake something. "Following directions is easy," thought Mia.

Mia found a cookbook and chose a recipe for a rich, gooey chocolate cake. She was excited. This was Mia's first attempt to bake by herself. She grabbed bottles, bags, and bowls. She mixed and poured at lightning speed. After the cake had baked, Mia cut herself a big slice. Ugh! It was the worst cake Mia had ever eaten. She must have used salt instead of sugar! So that she wouldn't make a mistake next time, Mia decided she would work slowly and carefully.

SKILL PRACTICE Read the item. Write your response.

1. Why did Mia decide to bake a cake by herself?

_____

_____

2. How did Mia's cake taste? Why?

_____

_____

3. What do you think Mia's face looked like when she bit into her cake?

_____

STRATEGY PRACTICE Tell a partner the beginning, middle, and end of the passage. Use one sentence to tell each part.

READ THE PASSAGE   Look for facts and opinions about the kudzu (KUD-zoo) plant.

The Ever-Growing Plant

What if you wanted to make a scary movie about a plant that grew out of control? What would that plant be like? Would it climb light poles and telephone wires? Would it wrap around trees and crawl all over fields? Would it climb tall buildings and cover a house until that house looks like a giant bush?

There is a plant like that in the southern United States. It's called kudzu, and it can grow a foot a day! Some people say if you stand still long enough, kudzu will grow all over you!

About 100 years ago, people liked kudzu. Farmers fed it to their cows. They planted it in their fields. The plant's strong roots kept the soil from washing away. People liked the shade the vines provided from the summer sun. After a time, people saw that nothing stopped kudzu from growing. The weather did not get cold enough to hurt the plant. Insects did not care to eat it. Now, people think kudzu grows too well. They think it is the worst plant in the world.

SKILL PRACTICE   Read the item. Write your response.

1. Write three facts from the article.

_____

_____

2. Which sentences in the last paragraph are opinions?

_____

3. Why did the author start the text with a series of questions?

_____

_____

STRATEGY PRACTICE   Underline the words or phrases that helped you form a good mental image of kudzu.

READ THE PASSAGE   Notice how the author organized each paragraph around a main idea.

Deep in the Sea

Deep in the sea, the water is almost black. The sun's rays do not reach down that far. Creepy creatures live in the dark ocean depths.

Some deep-sea fish create their own light so that they can see in the darkness. Chemicals in their bodies make their body parts glow. Some fish have rows of flashing lights along their bodies. Those lights scare off an attacker. Other fish have very long threads that grow from their jaw or lips. The threads end in a ball of light. These fish wiggle their lights to attract food. Curious fish swim to the light and become a meal. This is the best way to catch food.

Many deep-sea fish have huge mouths and teeth to help them catch fish. Gulper eels can unhook their jaws. It looks gross, but it lets their mouths open very wide. A viperfish has teeth that are so long and sharp that it can't close its mouth. Those teeth make a viperfish look scarier than a shark.

SKILL PRACTICE   Read the item. Write your response.

1. Which statement in the first paragraph is an opinion? Why?

_____

_____

2. How do lights help some deep-sea creatures and harm others?

_____

_____

3. List the two statements that are opinions in the last paragraph.

_____

STRATEGY PRACTICE   Underline one fact and draw a box around one opinion in each paragraph.

READ THE PASSAGE   Visualize how elephants use their trunks.

Terrific Trunks!

An elephant's trunk is the world's most useful nose. The trunk is used to drink, eat, smell, bathe, and greet other elephants!

Elephants use their trunks to help them find food and water. Because their noses are so large, elephants have a keen sense of smell. They can smell water or fruit that is miles away. An elephant can suck up two gallons (7.5 L) of water with its trunk. The elephant can squirt the water into its mouth if it's thirsty. It can squirt the water onto its back to cool down. The trunk wraps around branches and leaves. Then the elephant breaks off the food to put in its mouth. An elephant needs to eat about 300 pounds (135 kg) of grass, leaves, and fruit a day. So its trunk is very busy.

Elephants also use their trunks to show feelings. When two elephants meet, they may wrap their trunks in a "trunk-shake." Mother elephants pat their babies with their trunks. And baby elephants suck their own trunks for comfort.

SKILL PRACTICE   Read the item. Write your response.

1. How do elephants get and use water with their trunks?

_____

_____

2. Write three ways in which an elephant's trunk helps it to eat.

_____

_____

3. There is one opinion stated in the text. Write it and explain why it's an opinion.

_____

STRATEGY PRACTICE   Underline words and phrases in the passage that helped you visualize how elephants use their trunks.

Look for how African and Asian elephants are the same and different.

Be an Elephant Detective

Wrinkly gray skin, a huge body, a seven-foot (2-m) nose. Elephants all seem to look the same. But there are two different kinds of elephants—African and Asian. Each kind is named for the place where it lives in the wild. If you learn a few things to look for, you can tell whether an elephant is African or Asian.

An easy way to tell African and Asian elephants apart is to first look at an elephant's ears. An African elephant has large ears that flap like wings. An Asian elephant has much smaller, rounded ears. Next, look at the elephant's head. The top of an African elephant's head is rounded. But an Asian elephant's head has two bumps on it. If the elephant does not have tusks, it is a female Asian. Finally, check out the elephant's body. If the back dips down in the middle, it is an African elephant. The back of an Asian elephant is humped. If the two kinds of elephants stood side by side, the African elephant would be much larger.

SKILL PRACTICE Read the item. Write your response.

1. What is the text mainly about?

_____

_____

2. Name three ways in which African elephants differ from Asian elephants.

_____

_____

3. Name three ways in which African elephants are similar to Asian elephants.

_____

STRATEGY PRACTICE Write a question that you asked as you read the passage.

_____

READ THE PASSAGE Notice what makes the two sports the same and different.

Two Sports to Play

Soccer and basketball are sports that are alike in some ways. Both are played with a ball and two goals. In both sports, players dribble the ball to move it. Soccer players dribble the ball by moving it with their feet. They never use their hands. Basketball players dribble the ball by bouncing it with one hand. Players in both sports want to dribble the ball quickly. They don't want the other team to get it. They want to get the ball in the other team's goal and score.

A soccer ball is kicked to score points, so soccer goals are on the ground. They are tall and wide. A basketball, however, is thrown to score points. So basketball goals are placed high on poles.

Since basketballs and soccer balls are used in different ways, the sports are played on different kinds of surfaces. Soccer is played on grass, while basketball is played on a hard floor.

SKILL PRACTICE Read the item. Write your response.

1. What is the purpose of dribbling a ball in both sports?

_____

_____

2. How does scoring a goal in soccer differ from scoring a goal in basketball?

_____

_____

3. Write one sentence that sums up the use of hands and feet in these sports.

_____

STRATEGY PRACTICE Write a sentence that tells a difference between the two sports.

_____

  Daily Reading Comprehension • EMC 6363 • © Evan-Moor Corp.

Pay attention to what the passage says about Diego and his artwork.

Diego Rivera, Famous Artist

As a child, Diego Rivera drew everywhere. He drew on furniture, on walls, and across floors, too. So Diego's parents covered the walls of his room with sheets of paper. When he grew up, Diego became a famous muralist (MYOO-Ruhl-ist). A muralist is an artist who creates large drawings on walls.

Diego was born in Mexico. Some of his greatest murals are in Mexico City at the Office of Education. The building is two blocks long and one block wide. The walls are three stories high! Diego painted all the walls that faced the courtyard. He created 124 scenes about life in Mexico.

Diego's helpers began the project. They spread a paste called plaster on the walls. Then Diego painted the plaster. He used special paints that were made every day. Helpers made big buckets of the paint. Diego worked for five years painting all of the walls. He spent much of that time on ladders. He liked making art that was outdoors, where everyone could enjoy it.

SKILL PRACTICE Read the item. Write your response.

1. Why did Diego's parents cover the walls of his room with paper?

_____

_____

2. Why did the helpers make big buckets of paint daily?

_____

_____

3. What did Diego do in Mexico City? How was it similar to what he did as a child?

_____

STRATEGY PRACTICE With a partner, discuss one question you had as you read. Did you find the answer? If not, how could you find it?

Stop to tell yourself what is happening.

Lost in a Backpack

The class sat quietly. Some students stared out the windows and others doodled. Everyone was waiting for Max. He stood over his backpack, which was slumped on his desk. Max tugged at the zipper, which refused to budge at first. After a few more tries, Max unzipped his backpack. It was stuffed with things. "I know I put it in here last night," Max mumbled.

Max's teacher walked over to his desk and folded her arms. Her foot began a steady tap.

Max did not want to keep his teacher waiting. He reached into his backpack and quickly pulled out its contents. Out came gum wrappers and cookie crumbs. Out came rubber bands and markers. Out came some action figures and a broken pencil.

Max finally got to the bottom of the backpack. A sheet of paper wrinkled as he grabbed it. "I knew I would find it!" said Max. He sounded as if he had won a race.

SKILL PRACTICE Read the item. Write your response.

1. Describe how Max, his classmates, and his teacher feel at the start of the story.

_____

_____

2. What is on the sheet of paper that Max pulled out of the backpack?

_____

_____

3. "He sounded as if he had won a race." What did the author mean by this sentence?

_____

STRATEGY PRACTICE In five sentences or less, tell a partner what the passage is about.

READ THE PASSAGE Find out what is the same and different about goats and sheep.

Is It a Goat or a Sheep?

Goats and sheep seem very much alike. They both walk on two toes, which makes them very nimble animals. They can climb rocky ridges. And they can walk on narrow ledges like tightrope walkers in a circus. People around the world think both animals are good to eat and that their milk is good to drink. The milk of both goats and sheep is often made into cheese.

The bodies of sheep and goats are different. Most goats have beards, and most sheep do not. A goat's tail sticks up, while a sheep's tail hangs down. A goat's hair is short and stringy. The hair of a sheep is thick and curly and is called wool. It needs to be cut every year. The hair of both animals is made into yarn.

Goats and sheep have different behaviors, too. They both are grazers that eat plants. Sheep like to eat short, tender grass, while goats like to eat leaves, twigs, and vines. Goats can stand on their hind legs to reach food. Sheep like to stay together in flocks. But goats are more curious and independent than sheep.

SKILL PRACTICE Read the item. Write your response.

1. A woman is shaving an animal's coat. Is it a goat or a sheep? How do you know?

_____

2. How are the ways in which people use sheep and goats similar?

_____

3. An animal stands on its hind legs and chews a bush. Is it a goat or a sheep? Why?

_____

_____

STRATEGY PRACTICE Write a question you had and the answer you found in the passage.

_____

READ THE PASSAGE   Think about who this passage is about and where it takes place.

Diving Deep, Deep, Deep

Dr. Sylvia Earle is a scientist who studies the ocean. She studies fish and plants that live in the sea. Dr. Earle has discovered new sea life and has created underwater vehicles. She won a "Hero of the Planet" award for her efforts to protect the oceans.

Dr. Earle actually lived underwater for two weeks. She lived in a small lab on the ocean floor. The lab had four rooms in which the scientists ate and slept.

Dr. Earle set two deep-diving records. First, she made the deepest underwater walk. She wore a very heavy suit that was something like a spacesuit. The suit had a long cord that reached up to a boat. She wore a helmet that had four round windows in it so she could look forward, up, and out both sides. A few years later, Dr. Earle made a dive in a special vehicle made for deep dives. She broke the record for the deepest dive by a woman.

SKILL PRACTICE   Read the item. Write your response.

1. Picture Dr. Earle in the underwater lab. Is she alone? Explain.

_____

_____

2. What is Dr. Earle's main interest?

_____

3. Summarize Dr. Earle's achievements in two sentences.

_____

_____

STRATEGY PRACTICE   Write a sentence about a time when you explored.

_____

READ THE PASSAGE Visualize the sea lions.

Sea Animal Surprise

People usually go to the ocean to watch sea animals. But sometimes sea animals go to land to see people!

Monterey, California, is a city by the Pacific Ocean. California sea lions, which look like seals, live in those waters. Every day, sea lions are seen resting on rocks. In 2009, however, hundreds of barking sea lions waddled out of the ocean. They used their webbed flippers to scoot along. They moved up boat ramps and onto docks. Some even came onto a parking lot. A few checked out the restrooms.

Most of the sea lions that came ashore were tired from spending a long time looking for fish to eat. They plopped down to nap. A person was hired to get the sea lions back to their ocean home. He used a broom to shoo them back into the sea.

SKILL PRACTICE Read the item. Write your response.

1. What is the setting and who are the characters in this text?

_____

_____

2. Picture the sea lion "invasion" of 2009. Where do you see them?

_____

_____

3. Where do California sea lions spend their lives?

_____

_____

STRATEGY PRACTICE Underline words and phrases in the passage that helped you visualize where the sea lions were and what they did.

READ THE PASSAGE Think about what could and could not happen.

Make a Wish!

Carrie's party invitations had read, "Trot on over to my birthday party." Her girlfriends came by and had a lot of fun. They played pin the tail on the pony. They galloped around the yard like horses to see who was fastest. The girls made a craft, too. Carrie's mom brought out some real horseshoes. They were spray painted in bright colors. Each girl decorated a horseshoe with puffy paint and glitter. After that, the girls were ready for cake.

Carrie's cake was shaped like a horse with its front legs raised. Carrie's friends sang and then yelled, "Make a wish!" Carrie knew exactly what to wish for. She closed her eyes and thought about nothing but her wish. Then Carrie took a deep breath and blew out all nine candles. Poof! A pony appeared at Carrie's side. The pony inspected Carrie from head to toe. Then it flicked its tail and neighed. "I like your shoes, Carrie," it said. "Where can I get shoes that sparkle?"

SKILL PRACTICE Read the item. Write your response.

1. What did you picture in your mind when you read about the craft the girls did?

_____

_____

2. What can you infer about Carrie's interests based on her birthday party?

_____

_____

3. What two events in this story make it a fantasy?

_____

_____

STRATEGY PRACTICE Tell a partner about a wish you want to come true and why.

  Daily Reading Comprehension • EMC 6363 • © Evan-Moor Corp.

READ THE PASSAGE Think about what in the passage could happen and what is fantasy.

Yummy Clouds

The clock showed 3:58. Marco ran outside and gazed at the sky. Sure enough, clouds were gathering and blocking the sun. Clouds built up every Saturday at exactly this time. It was springtime, so the clouds were shaded in purple and orange. At 4:00, the clouds ripped open like bags. Marco smiled and held up his hands. Grape and cherry lollipops tumbled from the sky.

Marco stuffed his pockets with the treats. He liked the clouds in springtime. The polka-dotted clouds of summer were good, too. They tossed out blue, pink, and yellow jelly beans. In the fall, the clouds that gathered were deep red. Catching the long ropes of licorice was not easy. Dark brown clouds formed on Saturdays in the winter. Marco could almost smell the chocolate before it spilled out. Marco really liked living in Candy Land.

SKILL PRACTICE Read the item. Write your response.

1. Write the first sentence that let you know this was a fantasy. How did you know?

_____

_____

_____

2. Why does Marco enjoy living in Candy Land?

_____

_____

3. What does Marco look forward to getting from the clouds each fall?

_____

STRATEGY PRACTICE Describe the clouds you visualized to a partner.

READ THE PASSAGE   Visualize the events as you read. Think about what it means to be a friend.

What Is a Friend?

Long ago, Fox and Stork were friends. One evening, Fox invited Stork to his den for dinner. As a joke, Fox served a clear soup in a shallow dish. Fox easily lapped up his soup with his long tongue. But Stork's bill was long and narrow. It did not work like a straw. She could not eat her soup.

"I'm sorry you didn't like the soup," said Fox with a snicker. Before Stork left, she invited Fox for dinner the following night.

When Fox arrived at Stork's house, he smelled a delicious aroma. He hurried to the table. Stork had made a stew filled with meat and vegetables. Stork served the stew in two tall glass jars. She reached her long bill into her jar and gobbled it up. Fox's tongue could not reach the stew. "I'm sorry you didn't like the stew," said Stork.

Fox's stomach growled as he headed home. He knew he had treated Stork badly. That night he learned a lesson about friendship.

SKILL PRACTICE   Read the item. Write your response.

1. Could this story happen? Support your answer with two reasons.

_____

_____

2. How would you describe Fox? Why?

_____

3. What lesson about friendship does Fox learn from Stork?

_____

STRATEGY PRACTICE   Tell a partner how you feel when a friend is kind to you and when a friend is unkind to you.

READ THE PASSAGE Think about why the author wrote about these animals.

Animal Buddies

Some birds are friends of crocodiles. Other birds stay with hippos. One kind of bird visits badgers. These animals are partners. They help each other survive.

Crocodiles welcome small plover birds as guests. A croc opens its large jaw and the bird hops in. The plover nibbles the leftover food and the small animals stuck between the crocodile's teeth. As a result, the croc's teeth stay healthy, and the plover gets a meal.

It's not unusual to see an egret riding on a hippo's hide. Ticks and flies swarm around hippos. The bird doesn't have to move to get its food. The hippo gets rid of pests, and the egret gets to eat.

Some say that the honeyguide bird works with the honey badger. The bird flies to find a hive. It makes a racket when a hive is found. The badger hurries over and gets its fill of honey. The bird swoops down for the leftovers.

SKILL PRACTICE Read the item. Write your response.

1. How does a plover help a crocodile?

_____

_____

2. Why does an egret ride on a hippo's back?

_____

_____

3. What was the author's purpose for writing this text?

_____

STRATEGY PRACTICE What question did you ask yourself before you read?

_____

READ THE PASSAGE   Think about why the author wrote this passage.

Bring On the Snow!

You can make a snowy picture with snow that won't melt. First, get these supplies: colored poster board, various colors of construction paper, scissors, white glue, a plastic bowl, shaving cream, and a craft stick. Then follow these easy steps:

1. Think of a winter scene. Draw the objects of that scene on the sheets of construction paper. For example, draw your house and several trees.

2. Cut out the objects.

3. Glue the objects to the poster board to make a scene.

4. Stir together equal parts of shaving cream and white glue. Use the craft stick and the plastic bowl. You have made snow!

5. Use the craft stick to apply snow to the scene. You may want to put snow on the tree branches. You can make some snowmen with the snow, too.

6. Let the scene dry for an hour. The snow will be hard and puffy.

SKILL PRACTICE   Read the item. Write your response.

1. Why does the author include numbers in the passage?

_____

_____

2. What is used to make the "snow" for the picture?

_____

3. What was the author's purpose for writing this text?

_____

STRATEGY PRACTICE   Describe a snowy scene you have seen in real life or in a picture.

_____

_____

READ THE PASSAGE Visualize what is happening. Keep asking yourself what will probably happen next.

How High Can It Go?

Rey wants to build a tower. He is using things that he finds in his backyard.

Rey makes a patch of dirt flat. Then he begins making the base of his tower. Rey lays three bricks side by side. Then he places some flat rocks on top. Rey stacks more bricks on top of the rocks. The base is nice and strong.

Rey then spreads some grass on the flat rocks. Then he finds some twigs. He puts them in one layer. Rey sets more flat rocks on the twigs to keep them in place. The twigs look good poking out of the rocks. Then he finds some toy cars and lines them up on the rocks.

The tower is getting tall. Rey feels it's time to add some wood. He stacks three boards, then two bumpy rocks, and then three more boards. Rey saves the biggest and heaviest board for the top.

SKILL PRACTICE Read the item. Write your response.

1. What was the author's purpose for writing this text?

_____

_____

2. What did Rey do that was surprising?

_____

_____

3. What will probably happen next?

_____

STRATEGY PRACTICE Write a question you would ask Rey about building the tower.

_____

READ THE PASSAGE Think about other things Connor would probably do for his sister.

Big Brother Connor

Connor is always the last one to say good night to his little sister. After Mom kisses Katy, Connor chases away the bedroom monsters. He dances around the room and waves an imaginary wand. Connor shouts, "Alakazee! Alakazam! All you monsters flee to Amsterdam!" Then he tickles Katy's feet and tucks her in. Katy giggles as she says good night.

At breakfast, Connor pours cereal for Katy. When she spills her juice, Connor refills her cup. He tells her to eat all of her banana because it has lots of vitamins. After they eat, Connor helps Katy wash her hands. They brush their teeth together. "Let's pretend our brushes are trains," says Connor. "They're chugging down teeth tracks."

Katy puts on her coat all by herself when it is time to play. She and Connor storm out the door. "Play ball!" Katy begs. She points to a big, soft ball in the yard.

SKILL PRACTICE Read the item. Write your response.

1. Why does Connor run around Katy's room with an imaginary wand each night?

_____

_____

2. What do you think Connor probably did for Katy in the yard? Tell why.

_____

_____

3. What was the author's purpose for writing this text?

_____

STRATEGY PRACTICE With a partner, discuss whether or not you would like to have a brother like Connor.

READ THE PASSAGE Stop after each paragraph. Think of what the next paragraph is probably about.

How a Cut Becomes a Scab

You fall hard and cut your knee. Blood oozes from the broken skin. Before you can say "Ouch!" blood cells take action. Two important things happen.

Blood cells called platelets (PLAYT-lets) travel to the cut. The platelets stick together and help form a clot. The clot works like a bandage. It keeps more blood from flowing out. At the same time, white blood cells travel to the wound. They attack any germs that entered your body through the broken skin.

The bleeding stops, but your body continues to work. It makes new skin cells to repair the cut skin. The clot begins to dry and harden. A crusty, dark-red or brown scab forms. The scab allows the skin underneath to grow and heal. The scab also keeps germs from entering the wound. A scab falls off when the healing is complete. There's a fresh new layer of skin where the cut had been.

SKILL PRACTICE Read the item. Write your response.

1. What does the author compare the clot to in paragraph 2? Why?

_____

_____

2. Use information from the text to explain why you shouldn't remove a scab.

_____

_____

3. What was the author's purpose for writing this text?

_____

STRATEGY PRACTICE Write a question you still have about the passage.

_____

READ THE PASSAGE Pay close attention to the words in bold, or dark, print.

Listen Up!

Sound is energy that we hear. Sounds begin with vibrations. **Vibrations** are caused when something moves back and forth very quickly. Vibrations travel through the air in all directions. We call these vibrations **sound waves**.

Our ears have three parts. Each part has a special job to help us hear sounds. The **outer ear** is the only part that we can see. It catches sound waves that then travel to the **middle ear**. The middle ear sends the sound waves to the **inner ear**. The inner ear changes the sound waves into signals that go to our brains. That's when sound is heard. Hearing happens very quickly.

Almost every animal has a body part that hears. Not all animals' ears are like ours. Birds don't have outer ears, and their middle ears are covered by feathers. Snakes only have inner ears, which are connected to their jawbones. This allows snakes to feel vibrations from the ground, where tasty food might be living.

SKILL PRACTICE Read the item. Write your response.

1. Why are some words in the text in bold print?

_____

_____

2. How does the bold print help the reader understand the information?

_____

3. What kind of vibrations on the ground would interest a hungry snake?

_____

_____

STRATEGY PRACTICE How did the writer of the passage help you notice important ideas?

_____

READ THE INDEX Notice how the index is organized.

Using an Index

Use this index from the book *All About Pigs* to answer the questions.

Index	**All About Pigs**
barnyard 10	piglet 15, 16, 31, 34
bearded pig 28, 29	size 15, 28, 30, 33
giant forest hog 30–32	snout 5
hooves 7	tail 6
litter 15, 16	wart 28, 30, 33
mud bath 9, 10	wart hog 33–35
pig	
as food 11, 22–24	
as a pet 22, 25–27	

SKILL PRACTICE Read the item. Write your response.

1. What is the first page that has information about piglets? What is the last page?

_____

2. You just got a pig as a pet. What pages would you read first?

_____

3. What can you infer about giant forest hogs and wart hogs? Why?

_____

_____

STRATEGY PRACTICE How is an index arranged? Why?

_____

_____

Use the information to help you understand the graph.

Hearing Highs and Lows

Every sound has a **pitch**. The pitch of a sound is how high or how low the sound is. Study the graph. Each bar shows the lowest pitch to the highest pitch heard. The numbers are given in a measurement called hertz. Pitches over 20,000 hertz are too high for humans to hear.

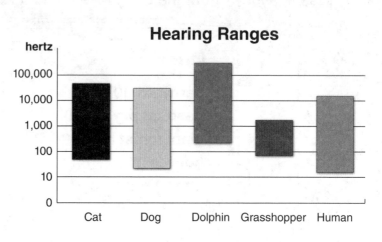

Hearing Ranges

Read the item. Write your response.

1. What is the purpose of this graph?

_____

_____

2. Which animal on the graph can hear the smallest range of pitches? How can you tell?

_____

_____

3. According to the graph, what is the hearing range for the average human?

_____

_____

Circle the sentence in the passage that is needed in order to understand the graph.

READ THE PASSAGE Think about how the illustration helps you understand time zones.

What Time Is It?

The world is divided into time zones. When you go from one time zone to another, the time changes. The map shows the time zones of the United States. In each zone, the time is one hour different from the zones next to it. Use the map to answer the questions.

United States Time Zones

11:00 AM — Hawaiian Time

12:00 PM — Alaskan Time — Alaska has two time zones.

1:00 PM — Pacific Time

2:00 PM — Mountain Time

3:00 PM — Central Time

4:00 PM — Eastern Time

SKILL PRACTICE Read the item. Write your response.

1. How many time zones are there in the entire United States?

_____

2. When it is 10:00 AM in the Mountain time zone, what time is it in the Eastern time zone?

_____

3. When it is 3:00 AM in the Central time zone, is it the same date in Hawaii? Explain.

_____

_____

STRATEGY PRACTICE How is a map a better way to find out about time zones than text? Talk about it with a partner.

READ THE PASSAGE   Notice the sentences that give the most important information.

What Everything Is Made Of

Matter is the material that makes up everything on Earth. Rocks, paper, wood, water, and even air are made of matter. Animals, plants, and people are made of matter, too. Matter is made up of very tiny parts called **atoms**. Atoms are too tiny to be seen. Atoms joined together in groups form molecules.

Matter exists in one of three basic forms: **solid**, **liquid**, or **gas**. For example, a pencil is a solid, milk is a liquid, and steam is a gas. Each of these forms has a different arrangement of molecules.

      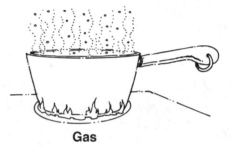

Solid   Liquid   Gas

SKILL PRACTICE   Read the item. Write your response.

1. How does the author let the reader know what the key terms for the topic are? Why?

_____

_____

2. Why did the text include the illustration?

_____

3. Look at the illustration. Explain how the molecules in a solid, a liquid, and a gas differ.

_____

_____

STRATEGY PRACTICE   Underline the sentence in the passage that helps you understand the illustration better.

READ THE PASSAGE Check to see that you understand the details as you read.

A Success Story

When Benjamin Carson was in fifth grade, he had the worst grades in his class. His mother decided things had to change. She made Benjamin read two library books a week. And he had to do book reports, too. His brain became excited by what he read. "My imagination went wild," said Benjamin. In a year, he was at the top of his class.

Today, Benjamin is Doctor Carson. He is one of the best brain surgeons in the country. He also wants to help kids to be the best they can be. He gives money to schools to create reading rooms, where kids can enjoy books. He also gives money to kids who come up with ways to help others.

Dr. Carson knows that the brain can do wonderful things. Dr. Carson says, "The brain remembers everything you've ever seen and everything you've ever heard. Whatever you can imagine, you can achieve." He knows this to be true. After all, Dr. Carson had once been at the bottom of his class.

SKILL PRACTICE Read the item. Write your response.

1. What is the first paragraph mostly about?

_____

2. Why did the author include the quotes from Dr. Carson?

_____

3. How did Benjamin help others after he grew up?

_____

_____

STRATEGY PRACTICE In your own words, write the main idea of the passage.

_____

READ THE PASSAGE Think about the story's beginning, middle, and end.

Spots, Bumps, and Blisters

Ginger woke up feeling itchy. She used her fingernails to scratch her tummy, her arms, and then her face. The itch still tingled. Ginger saw red bumps on her body. Had mosquitoes attacked her during the night? "Mom!" Ginger yelled.

Mom looked at her daughter's spotted body. "Looks like you've got chickenpox. I'll fill the bathtub with cool water and oatmeal. That should help stop the itching. And I'll get your mittens for you to wear afterward. You can't scratch those bumps."

"Take an oatmeal bath? Wear mittens in the summer? Can't scratch an itch? Chickenpox sure is weird," thought Ginger.

More spots appeared. There were too many to count. Before long, the bumps turned into blisters, and the blisters crusted with scabs. Ginger had to stay home. Her friends could not visit because they might get the chickenpox. Her best friend Mandy sent over a get-well gift. It was a big book of connect-the-dots.

SKILL PRACTICE Read the item. Write your response.

1. Which details help you to picture what Ginger's skin looks like and how it changes?

_____

_____

2. What is the second paragraph mostly about?

_____

_____

3. Why is it funny that Mandy gave Ginger a book of connect-the-dots?

_____

STRATEGY PRACTICE Give a summary of the passage in your own words.
Use three or four of the most important facts.

READ THE PASSAGE Think about the steps the spider takes to get its food.

Don't Fall for This Trap

There is a spider that is named for the way it catches its food. The sneaky trapdoor spider catches its prey with a hidden door.

The trapdoor spider first digs a burrow, or tunnel. It uses its fangs like a rake to move dirt. Next, it pulls silk threads from inside its body. It lines the burrow with the threads to make it smooth. Then, the spider begins to build a trapdoor. The spider mixes soil and silk to make a thick slab. It fits like a door over the opening to the burrow. Then, the spider covers the door with plants so it is hard to see. Now the spider is ready for a meal.

Bugs that crawl by make the ground vibrate, or move. The hairs on the spider's legs sense the vibrations. The spider pounces and carries its food down the burrow. Other trapdoor spiders stretch trip lines made from their silk. The spider feels the smallest twitch of the line. Out it rushes to get its meal.

SKILL PRACTICE Read the item. Write your response.

1. What is the purpose of the plants on the door?

_____

_____

2. What does the trapdoor spider use to form the door?

_____

_____

3. What is the trapdoor spider's first step in catching food?

_____

STRATEGY PRACTICE In your own words, describe to a partner how a trapdoor spider builds its burrow.

READ THE PASSAGE   Think about what is most important in making the treat.

A Treat on a Stick

Long ago, people made the first frozen treats. They mixed snow with some fruit, nuts, and honey. Today, kids around the world enjoy frozen treats on sticks. In some countries, the treat is called an ice pop. In other places, it's known as an icy lolly or ice block.

No matter what you call the treat, it's easy to make your own. And you don't need snow! Begin by pouring juice, or yogurt mixed with a little bit of juice, into small paper cups. Cover the top of each cup with foil. Cut a slit in the center of the foil. Next, poke a craft stick through the slit in the cup. Be careful not to create a big tear. If you do, replace the torn foil with a new piece.

Place the cups in the freezer until the juice freezes. Then peel off the foil. Quickly dunk the bottoms of the cups in hot water. That will make the pops easy to remove. Rinse the cups and let them dry. Then you can reuse the cups to make another batch.

SKILL PRACTICE   Read the item. Write your response.

1. What must you do in order to get the ice pop to slide out of the cup?

_____

_____

2. In which step does the writer encourage recycling?

_____

_____

3. What is the purpose of the foil?

_____

STRATEGY PRACTICE   Look back at the passage. Underline the sentences that are most important in making the frozen treats.

Daily Reading Comprehension • EMC 6363 • © Evan-Moor Corp.

READ THE PASSAGE Stop now and then to check that you understand what you read.

From Egg to Moth

Certain animals change as they grow from an egg to an adult. Each change is called a **stage**. The animal's body looks different during each stage. Moths, for example, go through four stages of changes.

A moth begins as an **egg**. The female moth lays eggs on the leaves or stem of a plant. The leaves will become food when the eggs hatch. An egg hatches into a **larva**, or caterpillar. The hungry caterpillar eats all the time. It grows and grows. Its skin becomes too tight. A new skin grows under the old skin. The old skin splits apart and is shed, or molted. Molting happens many times as the caterpillar grows. After the caterpillar molts for the last time, it fastens itself to a twig or leaf. Then it spins a cover called a cocoon over its body. This is the **pupa** stage. Inside the cocoon, the pupa is changing into an **adult**. The adult moth wiggles out of its cocoon. Its wings unfold and dry. The moth is ready to fly away.

SKILL PRACTICE Read the item. Write your response.

1. Write the main idea of this text in your own words.

_____

_____

2. What happens right after an egg hatches?

_____

_____

3. Your little brother shows you a cocoon. Explain to him what is happening.

_____

STRATEGY PRACTICE On the line, write words or facts from the passage that confused you.

_____

READ THE PASSAGE Think about the reasons why a bat hangs upside down.

Upside Down Works Best

A bat's body is small and light. It is built for flying. But it is also made for resting upside down. A bat's feet have toes that bend. The toes end in claws that are sharp and curved. Because bats have toes that bend and sharp claws, they can hold on tight to things. A bat's feet have special bones, too. Those bones lock into place when a bat hangs. This means that a bat can't fall, even when it rests.

Hanging upside down is useful for bats. Hanging high off the ground keeps bats safe from snakes and cats. And bats can live where other flying animals cannot. Unlike a bat, no bird can live on the ceiling of a cave. And not even a powerful bird like an eagle can hang upside down underneath a bridge.

Hanging also helps a bat fly. A bat's wings are about as thin as a plastic bag. They cannot lift a bat off the ground. However, hanging upside down is perfect for take-off. When a bat is ready to fly, it lets go, unfolds its wings, and glides away.

SKILL PRACTICE Read the item. Write your response.

1. List three places where you might find a bat hanging upside down.

_____

_____

2. Name two reasons why bats hang upside down.

_____

_____

3. Write the two sentences that tell why a bat doesn't fall when it sleeps.

_____

STRATEGY PRACTICE Describe a bat's feet to a partner, and tell how the feet help a bat hang upside down.

READ THE PASSAGE Think about how the author organized the information.

Rainforest Gliders

Some rainforest animals spend their lives in the treetops. All their food is right there. They never need to go to the ground. The tops of the trees in a rainforest form a kind of roof called a canopy. The fastest way to travel in the canopy is from tall tree to tall tree.

Some rainforest animals glide through the treetops in a special way. They use their skin! A flying squirrel has flaps of loose skin between its front and back legs. The squirrel jumps from a tree and spreads its legs. The skin stretches, and the squirrel flies like a kite. The flying gecko has flaps of skin along its body and tail. It jumps and then spreads the skin like wings. The gecko soars through the air. The flying frog has webbed feet that spread open like four umbrellas. They carry the frog through the air.

SKILL PRACTICE Read the item. Write your response.

1. Why do some animals spend their whole lives in the rainforest canopy?

_____

_____

2. What is similar about the three rainforest animals in the text?

_____

_____

3. Which of the animals in the text would you most like to see glide? Why?

_____

_____

STRATEGY PRACTICE Look back at the passage. Underline a sentence or phrase that tells a cause for something, and draw a box around the sentence or phrase that tells the effect.

Think about which statements are facts and which are opinions.

The Best Pets

Dogs make the best pets. They come in all sizes. Some dogs are as small as a football, and others are as tall as a desk. Dogs' fur is different, too. It can be tight with curls, long and silky, or smooth and stiff. The kind of fur does not matter, because all dogs are good to hug.

Dogs need to be groomed. Short-haired dogs are the easiest to care for. But all dogs need a bath once in a while. Giving a dog a bath is a lot of fun. When a dog is done getting bathed, it shakes the water off its body. Watch out or you will get wet!

Dogs like to please their owners, so dogs can be easy to train. They can follow simple commands and learn to walk on a leash.

Dogs truly are amazing animals. Some dogs pull sleds across icy places. Some save drowning people. Other dogs do tricks in movies. A dog has even flown in a rocket to outer space.

Read the item. Write your response.

1. How many opinions are stated in the first paragraph? How do you know?

_____

_____

2. How many facts does the author use in the last paragraph? How do you know?

_____

_____

3. Do you think the author owns a dog? Explain.

_____

Share with a partner what you visualized as you read the passage.

READ THE PASSAGE Think about how the student report is organized.

A Nice Place to Visit

I would like to explore the moon as an astronaut. It would be fun to wear a spacesuit and stomp on moon dust. The moon's gravity has a weaker pull than on Earth. I would be super strong! I could jump 12 feet (3.7 m) high and lift a 30-pound (17-kg) rock!

But I don't think the moon is a good place to live. Earth has an atmosphere, or a layer of gases. People, animals, and plants need these gases to live. The top layer of the atmosphere is our sky. The moon has no atmosphere, so it has no sky. It would be strange to see only stars and blackness.

Without air, nothing lives on the moon. I would miss trees and plants. And without air, there are no sounds on the moon. Silence all the time would be strange. I like the moon, but I'm not ready to live there.

SKILL PRACTICE Read the item. Write your response.

1. Describe Earth's atmosphere.

_____

_____

2. What is the first paragraph mostly about?

_____

3. There are two facts in the final paragraph. What are they?

_____

STRATEGY PRACTICE Write the main idea and one fact and one opinion from the second paragraph.

_____

_____

READ THE PASSAGE Visualize what you read about giraffes.

Giants of the Grasslands

Being 16 feet (5 m) tall can be a good thing. Giraffes can see far across the grasslands of Africa, where they live. They can be on the alert for hungry lions. Their height makes it easy to reach treetops for food.

To get enough food, giraffes have to eat nearly all day long. They eat about 75 pounds (34 kg) of leaves every day. Giraffes like to eat the thorny leaves of one kind of tree. Their saliva is amazing. It is thick like paste and protects their mouths from the thorns. And their thick lips act like cushions. A giraffe's tongue is interesting, too. It's about 20 inches (50 cm) long. The tongue is a dark blue-black color, so the hot sun does not burn it. The tongue wraps around food and grabs it the way you use your fingers and hand.

A big animal like a giraffe needs a big heart to pump blood through its body. A giraffe's heart weighs about 25 pounds (11 kg). And that's about the size of a beagle.

Everything about a giraffe is big!

SKILL PRACTICE Read the item. Write your response.

1. What is a giraffe's main predator? How do you know?

_____

_____

2. Why do giraffes have paste-like saliva and thick lips?

_____

_____

3. What does a giraffe spend most of its time doing? Why?

_____

STRATEGY PRACTICE Underline sentences in the passage that were easy to visualize.

READ THE PASSAGE Think of how an eagle's eyes and a person's eyes are alike and different.

Eyes Like an Eagle

Would you be surprised to learn that your eyes are like an eagle's eyes in some ways? You and an eagle can see colors. And an eagle's eyes and yours are about the same size. But there are a lot more of a special type of cell in an eagle's eyes than in your eyes. These cells send information to the eagle's brain. Getting a lot of information helps an eagle see much better than you. In fact, eagles can spot a fish in the sea from a mile (1.6 km) away.

You and an eagle have eyes that make tears. Your eyes make watery tears that clean your eyes. An eagle's eyes form watery tears *and* oily tears. Eagles dive into the sea to catch fish. The oily tears guard their eyes from the saltwater.

Like you, eagles have eyelids. You have two eyelids, and you close your eyes by lowering the top lid. When eagles close their eyes, their bottom lids raise up. Eagles have a third eyelid that moves across the eye every few seconds. It wipes dust away from the eye. An eagle can see through this third eyelid. The eyelid guards the bird's eyes when it swoops at 100 miles per hour (160 km per hour) after its prey.

SKILL PRACTICE Read the item. Write your response.

1. Name two ways in which an eagle's eyes are similar to yours.

_____

2. Name three ways in which an eagle's eyes are different from yours.

_____

_____

3. How does the way that an eagle blinks differ from the way that you blink?

_____

STRATEGY PRACTICE With a partner, share the question you wrote before you read the passage and tell whether you found the answer.

READ THE PASSAGE   Find out what is the same and different about Jenna and Eva.

It's Pizza Night!

Jenna and Eva are happy whenever their mom says it's pizza night. The sisters both love pizza. But they both are picky about the kind of pizza they like.

Jenna likes thick, chewy crust. Eva likes the crust to be thin and crispy. Eva and Jenna like tomato sauce on their pizza, but they prefer different toppings. Jenna likes plenty of cheese. Even if Jenna's pizza has three kinds of cheeses, she still sprinkles grated cheese on top. Eva likes pepperoni pizza that is not too spicy.

Eva's and Jenna's eating styles are different, too. Eva takes big bites of a pizza slice. She once ate a big slice in just four bites. Jenna folds a slice down the middle into a kind of pizza sandwich. She usually leaves a few bits of crust on her plate. Eva, however, eats every bite. Mom always hands a stack of napkins to both girls. Their faces are smeared with sauce by the end of the meal.

SKILL PRACTICE   Read the item. Write your response.

1. Which sister likes cheese better? What line in the text lets you know?

_____

_____

2. When you have pizza, is your eating style more like Jenna's or Eva's? Explain.

_____

_____

3. Why might it be difficult for the girls' mom to order a pizza?

_____

STRATEGY PRACTICE   Think of one similarity or difference between Eva and Jenna to write in a Venn diagram.

READ THE PASSAGE Stop after each paragraph and ask yourself questions about the information.

Marvelous Machines

Not so long ago, robots were machines seen only in movies. Today, robots are used all around the world. A robot is a special type of machine that can do some of the things a human can do. People invent robots in all shapes and sizes. No matter what they look like, all robots have a computer inside them. All robots can do two things. They can get information and they can move.

More and more robots are being invented. Some robots help people do tasks. Robots drill holes, spray paint, and put together cars. Robots help doctors perform operations. Robots drive trains and clean carpets.

Robots also go to places that are too dangerous for humans. Robots crawl through live volcanoes. They take samples of gases and examine the rocks. Robots dive deep into the oceans. They inspect strange sea creatures and collect items that have fallen to the ocean floor. Getting to Mars is not yet possible for astronauts, but robots have landed there. They collected rocks and took pictures.

SKILL PRACTICE Read the item. Write your response.

1. What three facts apply to all robots?

_____

2. How have robots helped humans learn more about science? Why?

_____

_____

3. What prediction can you make about robots in the future?

_____

STRATEGY PRACTICE What question did you ask yourself about the third paragraph?

_____

READ THE PASSAGE Look for clues that tell you about Sean.

Not-So-Speedy Sean

The third-graders call Sean "Speedy." When Sean gets to school, he hurries out of the car. He runs up the stairs two at a time. And he comes to a sliding stop just outside the classroom door. Sean is the first one out the door at recess. He always eats his snack while heading to the playground. When the bell rings to come in, Sean beats everyone back to class.

Last week, Sean dragged his feet into the classroom. At recess, he sat on a playground bench. Sean gave his snack to a friend. Sean's shoulders drooped, and his head hung down. His nose leaked like a dripping faucet. He coughed with a rumble.

Sean's teacher noticed his unusual behavior. She wondered if he had a fever. She walked over to the bench where Sean sat. She placed her hand on Sean's forehead and then sent him to the school office. Sean was snoring softly when his dad arrived to take him home.

SKILL PRACTICE Read the item. Write your response.

1. How did Sean get the nickname "Speedy"? Give an example from the text.

_____

_____

2. Why did Sean's dad come to school?

_____

_____

3. What will Sean probably do when he gets home?

_____

STRATEGY PRACTICE Tell a partner how you stayed focused on what you were reading.

READ THE PASSAGE   Think about the differences between lions and tigers.

Big, Wild Cats

The roar of a lion or a tiger can make a person shake with fear. These big cats live in the wild, but they live in different places in the world.

Lions live in the grasslands of Africa. Their sandy-colored fur blends with the tall, yellow grasses. Tigers live in forests and jungles in Asia. Their orange fur has dark stripes that help tigers hide among the trees. The weather is hot where lions and tigers live. Lions try to stay dry, but they will go into the water if they have to. Tigers like to cool off in water. Both kinds of big cats live and hunt in an area that covers many miles. This is their territory. Lions live in groups called prides. Each pride has its own territory. A tiger lives alone in its territory.

Lions and tigers are strong hunters with sharp teeth and claws. Both kinds of big cats are meat eaters. They both tend to creep up to their prey and attack by surprise. Lions hunt in small groups, but a tiger hunts by itself.

SKILL PRACTICE   Read the item. Write your response.

1. Name three ways in which lions and tigers differ.

_____

_____

2. Name three ways in which lions and tigers are alike.

_____

_____

3. How does each big cat's fur help it to blend in with its surroundings?

_____

_____

STRATEGY PRACTICE   Think of a question about the passage and have a partner answer it.

READ THE PASSAGE Find out how a zoo doctor does her job.

Working with Wild Things

How do you give a fish a pill? How do you help a hurt giraffe? Dr. Cheryl Cullion (KUHL-lee-un) knows. She is a zoo doctor. She cares for nearly 1,000 animals. She has patients that growl, swing, and stomp. And all of her patients are wild.

Giving zoo animals their medicine can be difficult. Some animals just eat their pills. Others need to be tricked. Dr. Cullion knows what works. She hides pills in the fish that penguins eat. She adds a cherry flavor to the medicine for monkeys. To help fish, she quickly stuffs a pill into their gills.

Being a zoo doctor is a challenging job. Dr. Cullion once had to check the health of monkeys that were new to the zoo. She needed to watch them to make sure that they ate. But there was a problem. All of the monkeys looked alike! So the doctor made some safe colors from vegetables. She dyed each monkey's fur a different color. Then she could tell them apart. They were punky monkeys!

SKILL PRACTICE Read the item. Write your response.

1. What is the setting for this text? How do you know?

_____

_____

2. Why did the zoo doctor dye the monkeys' fur?

_____

_____

3. Does Dr. Cullion like wild animals? Explain your reasoning.

_____

STRATEGY PRACTICE Tell a partner what you know about animal doctors.

READ THE PASSAGE   Who or what is the passage about, and where does it take place?

Go Away!

Bo sat quietly out of sight. The scientist was watching a porcupine climb down a pine tree. About 30,000 quills covered the porcupine's back and tail. The quills, which are stiff hairs, lay flat against the animal's body.

Then Bo heard a noise. So did the porcupine. A hungry coyote wandered out of the woods. The porcupine's quills stood up. The scared porcupine gave a warning by stamping its feet. The coyote did not move. The porcupine shook its tail so the quills rattled. Still the coyote did not move.

Bo wondered how the porcupine would defend itself. He knew the porcupine could not shoot its quills. That happened only in cartoons. Then the porcupine turned its back end to the coyote. It slapped the coyote with its tail. At the same time, the porcupine moved some muscles. That released many quills. Some quills stuck right in the animal's hide. The coyote left with a whimper. Losing the quills was no problem for the porcupine. They would grow back.

SKILL PRACTICE   Read the item. Write your response.

1. Are the animal characters in the text friends? How do you know?

_____

_____

2. Describe where the action is taking place.

_____

3. Are coyotes easy to frighten? How can you tell?

_____

_____

STRATEGY PRACTICE   Look back at the passage. Underline the words or phrases that helped you visualize what you read.

READ THE PASSAGE Think about what can happen and what cannot happen.

Professor, the Cat

Rosa's cat, Professor, looked like an ordinary cat. His fur was striped in gray and black, and his eyes were yellow and round. Professor meowed and scratched like most cats. And he liked to chase anything that moved.

One night, Professor sat on Rosa's desk. He watched Rosa struggle with her homework. Rosa yawned and rubbed her eyes. She could not stay awake to finish her homework. Rosa left the paper on her desk. She scratched Professor behind his ears and said good night. Soon, Rosa was fast asleep and softly snoring.

Professor looked at the arithmetic homework. With a proud meow, Professor picked up a pencil. The cat used his toes to count. The cat wrote in the answers and completed the page. Then Professor looked at Rosa and smiled. He liked being Rosa's friend.

SKILL PRACTICE Read the item. Write your response.

1. Why is Professor a good name for Rosa's cat?

_____

_____

2. Is this story real or make-believe? What is the first sentence that let you know for sure?

_____

_____

3. How do you think Rosa felt when she woke up and saw her homework? Explain.

_____

_____

STRATEGY PRACTICE Tell a partner what you would have Professor do for you.

READ THE PASSAGE   Keep track of all the things you read that could <u>not</u> happen.

The Attack of the Giant Mosquitoes

This is a story about Paul Bunyan, the most famous lumberjack of all time. Bunyan was as tall as a mountain. He could chop down 100 trees with one mighty swing of his ax. It is a fact that he and his men cut down every tree in Texas. All that grows in that state nowadays is wheat.

One day, Paul's men were in the woods when a hungry swarm of mosquitoes attacked. The pests were as big as eagles. They zoomed in on the men and bit them all. Before long, the men were full of holes. They looked like window screens or pieces of Swiss cheese.

The mosquitoes then dared to attack Bunyan. He held a frying pan as big as a football field over his head. *Wham!* The mosquitoes slammed into the pan. Their stingers went right through it. The bugs couldn't shake the pan loose, so they buzzed off with it. The pests were mighty tired by the time they flew over Lake Michigan. The giant mosquitoes splashed into the lake. The pan pulled them under the water. That was the last anyone saw of them.

SKILL PRACTICE   Read the item. Write your response.

1. Write the one sentence from the text that could really happen.

_____

2. Using the information in the first paragraph, explain what a lumberjack is.

_____

3. What probably happened to the mosquitoes in Lake Michigan? Explain.

_____

_____

STRATEGY PRACTICE   Draw a picture of something you visualized as you read the passage.

READ THE PASSAGE   Visualize the main character, the setting, and events.

Messy Jessie

Jessie stomps into her room. She got home late from school. Now she has just a few minutes to get ready for soccer practice. Jessie pulls off her green sweatshirt and tosses it on the floor. "Hey! Watch it!" the sweatshirt yells.

Then Jessie flings her cap. "Ouch!" it shouts. The bedroom floor is always piled with clothes. Jessie steps all over them while looking for her soccer shirt. She doesn't hear the moans and groans.

Then Jessie kicks off her purple shoes. She watches them sail through the air. Each shoe lands with a thump. "Oof! Ow!" scream the shoes.

Jessie plops onto the floor. She tears off her red socks and rolls each into a ball. With a quick toss, Jessie plunks the socks into her wastebasket. The socks complain. "Hey! Where are we? It's dark in here!"

Jessie dresses and dashes out of her room. "We've got to speak up," begs the sweatshirt. "It's time to tell Jessie to take better care of us."

SKILL PRACTICE   Read the item. Write your response.

1. Use details from the text to describe the setting.

_____

_____

2. Who is the main character, and what can you tell about the person?

_____

_____

3. Who is the sweatshirt talking to in the last paragraph? Why?

_____

STRATEGY PRACTICE   Tell a partner how your room compares to Jessie's room.

READ THE PASSAGE Think about why the author wrote the passage.

Hairy Eggshells

While eggs are a favorite food all around the world, the eggshells are usually thrown away. But you can turn them into seed pots. You need: eggs, markers, a sponge cut into small pieces, some grass or alfalfa seeds, and an egg carton. Then follow these simple steps:

1. Carefully crack each egg into two parts. Try to make one part a lot bigger than the other. Throw away the smaller part. Save the insides, and use them later for cooking.
2. Rinse out the eggshells. Let them dry.
3. Draw faces on the outsides of the dry eggshells.
4. Wet each sponge piece. Place a sponge inside each eggshell.
5. Sprinkle some seeds on top of the sponges.
6. Use the egg carton to hold the eggshells.
7. Water the eggshells lightly every day. The seeds will sprout in about one week, and the eggshell faces will have green hair!

SKILL PRACTICE Read the item. Write your response.

1. Why did the author write this text?

_____

_____

2. How does the numbered list help the reader understand what to do?

_____

3. Do you think this text could be improved if it had an illustration? Why or why not?

_____

STRATEGY PRACTICE Write a question using information you read in the passage.

_____

READ THE PASSAGE   Think about why the author wrote the passage.

A Small Beginning

Trees grow larger than other plants, including flowers and bushes. And yet, most trees begin as tiny seeds.

The seed is the first stage in a tree's growth. A seed has a hard shell that protects the plant inside. When the plant is ready to grow, it sprouts, or pushes out of the seed. The new, small plant is called a **seedling**. The seedling needs air, light, and water to grow. It also needs to be planted in good soil.

As the seedling gets bigger, it looks more like a tree. The shoot, or stem, of the seedling grows into a **sapling**. This young tree grows bark on its trunk and leaves on its branches. The sapling will continue to grow until it is a large tree.

All seeds have a built-in code. Tree seeds have a code that tells seedlings the kind of tree they will become. For example, an acorn will grow into an oak tree. A pine seed will grow into a pine tree. The size of the seed has nothing to do with how tall a tree grows. The code inside the seed determines a tree's type and size.

SKILL PRACTICE   Read the item. Write your response.

1. Why did the author write this text?

_____

_____

2. Why did the author put some words in bold print?

_____

3. What four things does a seedling need in order to grow into a sapling?

_____

STRATEGY PRACTICE   Describe a connection you made when you read the passage.

_____

READ THE PASSAGE   Look for information that will help you know what will happen next.

From Baby to Big

The eggshells cracked open. Baby birds with skin as pink as watermelon sat in the nest. They could not see, and they could not walk. All they could do was open their beaks wide. Their parents flew back and forth to the nest every few minutes. The babies, or **nestlings**, depended on their parents for food.

In a few days, the nestlings changed. Soft gray down covered their skin. The birds looked like small balls of fuzz. They could see, but they could not fly. They could not even hop. Days later, the down fell out. Feathers grew in to help them fly.

The young birds were now **fledglings**. They were getting ready to fly away. Their bodies were bigger, and they were hungry for more food. Some of the fledglings hopped, and others fluttered their wings. Their mother taught them sounds to make. She knew they would try to leave the nest. She taught them to make a sound when they needed help.

One day, a fledgling stood on the rim of the nest. It flapped its wings hard.

SKILL PRACTICE   Read the item. Write your response.

1. What will happen next in the story?

_____

_____

2. After the baby birds hatch, why do the parents return to the nest every few minutes?

_____

_____

3. When does a nestling turn into a fledgling? How do you know?

_____

_____

_____

STRATEGY PRACTICE   Write the question you thought of before you read the passage.

_____

Stop after each paragraph and ask yourself what will likely happen next.

Saturday Fun

Dad and Rusty have a Saturday routine. They play catch in the morning. Around noon, Rusty heads out her dog door. She walks into the yard to her favorite spot under the oak tree. The grass there is smashed flat from her body. Rusty turns around three times and then lands with a sigh. She curls up in the grass and lays her head on her paws. She begins snoring in less than a minute.

Dad watches a ballgame for a few hours. Then he glances at his watch and gets up from the chair. Dad pats his pants' pocket to make sure his house keys are inside. Then he walks to the kitchen and opens a drawer. He drags out a long red leash and he whistles.

Rusty's head pops up like a jack-in-the-box. She knows what that whistle means. Rusty dashes through her dog door and stops in front of Dad. Her tail wags as she looks up at Dad. She likes seeing the leash in his hand.

SKILL PRACTICE Read the item. Write your response.

1. What will Dad and Rusty do next? How do you know?

_____

_____

2. Based on Rusty's name, what do you think she looks like?

_____

_____

3. How does Rusty feel about the leash? Support your answer with text evidence.

_____

STRATEGY PRACTICE Share with a partner what you know about dogs and the things they can do.

READ THE PASSAGE Ask yourself why the author wrote this and what will happen next.

Carla's Treasures

Carla didn't walk fast. She kept her eyes looking at the ground. Carla was always on the lookout for treasures. Her dad had built a bookcase to hold what Carla found. She had carefully organized the things.

The top shelf held bird treasures. Most items were feathers that Carla had found. Some were wing feathers and some were tail feathers. A nest of grass, string, and twigs lay at the end of the shelf. It had fallen from a tree in the park. Rocks and stones sat on the middle shelf. A few rocks were black and were made by volcanoes. Some of the pebbles were shiny. The bottom shelf held a variety of things. There were a few bones that were probably from a chicken. And there was a long piece of skin a lizard had shed.

Carla cleared a space on the bottom shelf. Today she was going to the beach!

SKILL PRACTICE Read the item. Write your response.

1. What was the author's purpose for writing this text?

_____

_____

2. In what way are all of Carla's treasures alike?

_____

3. What "treasures" do you think Carla will find at the beach?

_____

STRATEGY PRACTICE What are some questions you would ask Carla about her treasures?

_____

_____

Look for important details about the spiny anteater.

Quite a Creature

A Strange Mammal

An echidna (ee-KID-nuh) is a spiny anteater. It belongs to a group of mammals called monotremes (MON-oh-treemz). This means it can lay eggs!

An echidna mother lays one egg. She warms it in a pouch on her stomach. A baby hatches around ten days later. It's called a puggle (PUHG-uhl). It's about the size of a jelly bean. Once the puggle grows spines, it's sent out of the pouch!

All Nose and Tongue

The echidna eats ants and termites. It pokes its long, thin snout into ant nests and termite homes. Then its long, sticky tongue reaches into the nest. The bugs stick to the tongue like gum to a shoe. Grains of dirt stick to the tongue, too. But the dirt is not a problem. An echidna does not have teeth. The dirt does the work of teeth and grinds the bugs so they can be swallowed.

SKILL PRACTICE Read the item. Write your response.

1. How does a monotreme differ from most mammals?

_____

2. Why does a pronunciation in parentheses immediately follow some of the words?

_____

_____

3. What illustration could improve this text? How would it help readers?

_____

_____

STRATEGY PRACTICE Discuss with a partner how the subheads help you notice what is important.

READ THE GLOSSARY Notice how the words from a book on geography are organized.

Glossary

canyon a deep, narrow valley with steep sides

city a very large town

coast land that is next to an ocean or a sea

coastline where the land and an ocean meet

community a group of people who live together in the same area

compass rose a symbol that shows directions on a map

culture a way of life, ideas, customs, and traditions

custom a way of acting; something done regularly

degree a unit for measuring temperature

desert dry land that gets little or no rain

ecosystem a community of plants and animals

equator an imaginary line that runs around the middle of Earth

SKILL PRACTICE Read the item. Write your response.

1. Which word describes all the plants and animals living in a desert? How do you know?

_____

2. Between which two entries in this glossary would the entry for *Celsius* go? Why?

_____

_____

3. You come to the unknown word *equator* and turn to the glossary. What does it tell you?

_____

_____

STRATEGY PRACTICE How is the information in a glossary organized?

_____

READ THE PASSAGE   Read the passage and study the circle graph.

A Simple Survey

Juan's teacher asked the students to raise their hands if they had a pet. Juan was surprised to see that everyone raised their hands. So he took a survey. Juan made a circle graph and a key to show what he found out.

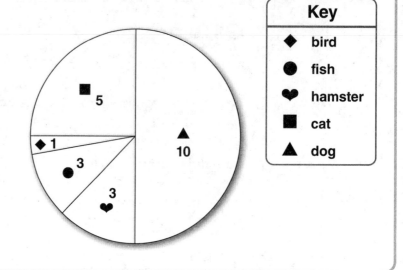

Key	
◆	bird
●	fish
♥	hamster
■	cat
▲	dog

SKILL PRACTICE   Read the item. Write your response.

1. What information is given in the key?

_____

_____

2. Which two types of pets are owned by the same number of students? How do you know?

_____

_____

3. How many students own a cat?

_____

STRATEGY PRACTICE   Could you understand the circle graph if the key was missing? Explain your answer.

_____

_____

READ THE PASSAGE Find out what information is given in the passage and what information is given in the graph.

Treats from Trees

Chocolate trees do exist. They are called cocoa trees. Pods shaped like footballs hang from the trees. The pods hold very bitter beans. Workers and machines turn the beans into sweet chocolate. People all around the world love to eat chocolate.

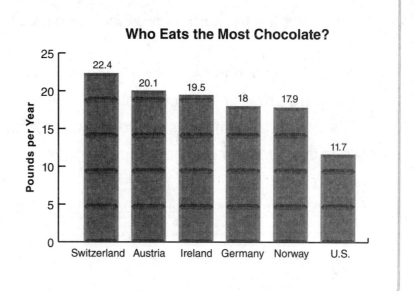

Who Eats the Most Chocolate?

SKILL PRACTICE Read the item. Write your response.

1. Do people eat chocolate right off the tree? How can you tell?

_____

_____

2. How many nations are shown on the graph, and what are their names?

_____

_____

3. What kind of information is given in the text but NOT the graph?

_____

_____

STRATEGY PRACTICE Name two ways that information is presented in the selection.

_____

READ THE PASSAGE   Be aware of the most important information.

Pushed to the Top

Fossils are the hardened remains of plants or animals that lived long ago. Fossils are found buried in rock. The fossils of some ocean animals that lived millions of years ago have been found on mountains! How did they get there?

Earth's **crust**, or surface, is always moving. This movement builds mountains. As large pieces of the crust move, they sometimes **collide**, or run into each other. When this happens, rock layers push together and move up. Sometimes, the layers are pushed up all the way from the ocean floor. If those rock layers contained fossils, the fossils moved up with the rocks.

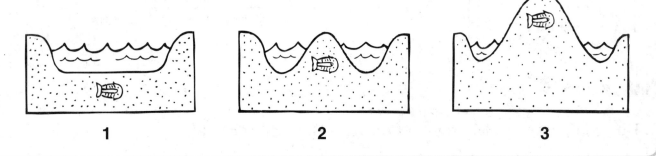

1   2   3

SKILL PRACTICE   Read the item. Write your response.

1. How do the illustrations support the text?

_____

_____

2. Why are the illustrations numbered?

_____

3. Why did the author put some of the words in the text in boldface?

_____

STRATEGY PRACTICE   Underline the words or phrases in the passage that helped you understand what the vocabulary words mean.

READ THE PASSAGE   Stop after each paragraph and think about what the paragraph said.

Made to Live in Water

People breathe air and so do dolphins. They breathe through an opening in the top of their head. The opening is called a blowhole. The blowhole is a flap of skin that can open and close. When a dolphin swims to the water's surface, it uses strong muscles to open its blowhole. The blowhole closes as a dolphin dives back underwater.

People do not have to think about breathing while they sleep. Breathing happens automatically. A dolphin must be awake to control its blowhole. And it needs to rest. How can it breathe *and* rest? When a dolphin rests, it swims slowly. Half of its brain shuts down. The other half stays alert for danger. It also signals the dolphin when to rise out of the water for a breath of air. After a couple of hours, the halves of the dolphin's brain trade jobs.

SKILL PRACTICE   Read the item. Write your response.

1. Write the main idea of the text in your own words.

_____

_____

2. What part of the human body is a dolphin's blowhole most like?

_____

_____

3. When it comes to breathing, how does a dolphin's brain differ from the human brain?

_____

_____

STRATEGY PRACTICE   Tell a partner how a dolphin breathes while it rests.

READ THE PASSAGE   Notice which events are important.

Get Ready! Get Set!

Before I went to bed, I checked and rechecked my clothes for the Fourth of July parade. Mom had washed and ironed my Girl Scout uniform. It was clean and crisp. I made sure every badge was sewn on tightly. And I looked for scuff marks on my shoes. Our leader, Mrs. Murray, wanted our troop to look perfect. The parade route was a mile long, so many people would see us. Some of the girls in my troop were going to play the drums. We had practiced marching to their beat.

The morning of the parade was a mad scramble around our house. I was dressed an hour ahead of time. But Dad was looking for picnic chairs. Mom was packing snacks. Our dog Fudge wanted to play, so he grabbed a small bag of chips. He dashed away whenever Mom got near. Mom's voice grew louder and louder as she chased Fudge. He finally dropped the chips when I offered him a doggy treat.

We hurried to the car. I sat with a smile. In my mind, I could picture the crowd cheering as I marched by.

SKILL PRACTICE   Read the item. Write your response.

1. Why is the author so excited?

_____

_____

2. Write the three most important details about the parade.

_____

3. What two events happen that delay the family from leaving the house?

_____

STRATEGY PRACTICE   Underline the sentence in each of the first two paragraphs that tells the main idea.

Daily Reading Comprehension • EMC 6363 • © Evan-Moor Corp.

READ THE PASSAGE   Pay attention to the steps used in making shoes long ago.

Shoes from Long Ago

Long ago, people owned only one or two pairs of shoes. They were made by a shoemaker who used hides, or skins, of horses, cows, pigs, or goats.

Making a pair of shoes could take days. The shoemaker first measured a person's feet. He then chose the wooden, foot-shaped form that was the right size. This form was called a *last.* The shoemaker stretched a piece of hide over each last to shape the shoes. He used the lasts to cut the soles and heels, too. These were cut out of the thickest part of the hide.

Strong tools were needed to sew the parts of the shoes together. The shoemaker used an awl to punch holes in the pieces. He then used a stiff hog hair as a needle. The shoemaker sewed the top parts of the shoes to the soles. He then cleaned and polished the shoes. Finally, the shoemaker nailed on the heels. Before brass nails came into use, the heels were held on with wooden pegs.

It's no wonder that a shoemaker was an important man in a village!

SKILL PRACTICE   Read the item. Write your response.

1. Why does the shoemaker use a last?

_____

_____

2. What three signal words help guide the reader through the text?

_____

_____

3. What is the final step in making a pair of shoes?

_____

STRATEGY PRACTICE   Look back at the passage. Number the first four steps in making shoes long ago.

READ THE PASSAGE Focus on the most important information.

Inside a Seed

Seeds are everywhere. They can glide through the air or hitch a ride on an animal's fur. Seeds come in different shapes and sizes. But they are the same in one way. Inside each seed is the beginning of a new plant. Take a look inside a bean to see for yourself.

First, get several dried beans such as lima beans or pinto beans. Notice how hard the beans feel. Now, place the beans in a container and cover them with water. Let the beans soak overnight. They are bigger and softer now. Next, gently peel off the seed coating. This covering protects the baby plant inside, just as a jacket protects you from the cold. Then, open the bean into its two halves. With a magnifying lens, you can see the little plant that is waiting to grow. Do you see a root and tiny leaves? Around the tiny plant is food. It will use this food as it sprouts and starts to grow. Finally, plant the other beans in potting soil and watch them become bean plants.

SKILL PRACTICE Read the item. Write your response.

1. How does the author say you can soften lima beans?

_____

_____

2. What can you see with a magnifying glass?

_____

3. In what way do seeds differ?

_____

_____

STRATEGY PRACTICE Draw a box around the words in the passage that signal steps in a sequence.

Daily Reading Comprehension • EMC 6363 • © Evan-Moor Corp.

Think of questions you have about the information.

The Buzz About Honeybees

What animals live in homes filled with sweet, sticky stuff? Honeybees! Honeybees and people both like to eat honey. Honeybees do the work that makes this sweet food.

To make honey, honeybees need a lot of nectar. Nectar is a kind of sugar water found inside flowers. First, a worker bee lands on a petal. She uses her long tongue to sip the nectar. She stores the nectar in a special honey stomach. That stomach is different from her regular stomach. She may make hundreds of stops before her honey stomach is full. Next, the bee flies her heavy load back to the hive. Then, she spits up the nectar. Another worker bee chews on the nectar for quite a while. Then, she puts the sticky stuff into a wax cell of the honeycomb. More worker bees fan their wings to help dry the nectar. As it dries, it gets very sticky. Finally, the sugars turn into honey for the bees to eat.

All of these worker bees do their jobs over and over. It takes a lot of nectar to make enough honey to feed the thousands of bees in the hive.

SKILL PRACTICE Read the item. Write your response.

1. Do male or female honeybees gather nectar? How do you know?

_____

_____

2. When and how do the bees dry the nectar?

_____

3. Does a single honeybee visit only a few flowers? What text evidence lets you know?

_____

_____

STRATEGY PRACTICE Tell a partner the important steps in making honey.

READ THE PASSAGE   Look for causes and effects.

Useful Dead or Alive

A living tree is a wonderful gift of nature. Trees breathe out oxygen, refreshing the air. Trees give cool shade to plants, people, and animals. Many animals make their homes in trees, too. The fruits and nuts of some trees are tasty foods for both people and animals.

A tree is important even after it dies. Insects and birds depend on the dead wood. Some birds nest in the holes of the tree. Bees and wasps might make homes there, too. Some insects lay their eggs in the bark. Birds swoop by and eat the plump larvae.

Fungi (FUHN-jye), or mushrooms, grow on the dead wood. They begin to decompose the tree. They cause the tree to rot. Soft green moss and various bacteria, or germs, grow there, too. They all help the tree to rot. The tree gets softer and more crumbly. The rotting is important. As the tree rots completely, it makes the soil rich. The soil will be just right for new plants to grow.

SKILL PRACTICE   Read the item. Write your response.

1. This is the effect: The dead tree decomposes. Name the causes.

_____

2. This is the cause: A dead tree completely breaks down. Name the effects.

_____

_____

3. Describe the benefits offered by a living fruit tree.

_____

_____

STRATEGY PRACTICE   Circle words and phrases from the passage that helped you visualize what you read.

Daily Reading Comprehension • EMC 6363 • © Evan-Moor Corp.

READ THE PASSAGE Find the main idea of each paragraph.

Under Ice

Winter storms can cause big problems. One of the worst kinds of storms is an ice storm. Certain conditions cause ice storms. The air closest to the ground must be very cold. The air layer above the ground must be warm. And the highest layer of air must be cold. Snow from the top cold layer falls into the warm air layer and starts to melt. Those water drops continue to fall through the bottom cold layer. If the temperature is below freezing, the drops refreeze quickly. They coat everything in ice. The freezing rain can last for hours. The ice builds and gets very heavy.

Ice storms result in danger and damage. Highways and roads are extremely slippery. The heavy ice makes power lines break and fall. Then people do not have electricity. Plants die if they are coated with ice for a long time. Animals cannot get to the plants that are frozen in ice. Birds lose their homes when tree branches crack. There's nothing good about an ice storm.

SKILL PRACTICE Read the item. Write your response.

1. What are two results (effects) of an ice storm?

_____

_____

2. Write the sentence in the first paragraph that states the main idea of the paragraph.

_____

_____

3. Picture the snow falling and changing until it forms ice on branches. Describe the steps.

_____

_____

STRATEGY PRACTICE Draw an X beside the paragraph that tells about the effects of ice storms.

READ THE PASSAGE Which statements about ostriches can be proved true?

Big and Bold

An ostrich is not an ordinary bird. It is the largest and heaviest bird. It has beautiful long feathers, but it cannot fly. Because of its size, an ostrich is built for running. It can take giant steps. It can sprint like a runner, too. Even the bird's wings help it run. If an ostrich needs to dash away, it spreads its wings. The wings keep the ostrich balanced. The wings also help an ostrich make sharp turns to confuse its enemy. It is a remarkable bird!

The most dangerous parts of an ostrich are its toes. The ostrich is the only bird with two toes on each foot. The longer of the toes ends in a four-inch claw. These claws can tear into an animal's hide. And the ostrich's strong legs can give a powerful kick.

Although an ostrich eats mostly plants, it will also eat whatever it can find. It will eat insects and small animals such as lizards. Pebbles and dirt are part of its diet, too. An ostrich does not have teeth. Swallowing small stones and dirt helps an ostrich to grind up the food. That makes the food easier to digest.

The ostrich is a very strange bird indeed!

SKILL PRACTICE Read the item. Write your response.

1. Are there any opinions in the first paragraph? Explain.

_____

_____

2. Are there any facts in the second paragraph? How do you know?

_____

3. If you looked in an ostrich's stomach after it had eaten, what could you find there?

_____

STRATEGY PRACTICE Tell a partner which part of the passage was easiest to visualize.

READ THE PASSAGE Notice what each paragraph is about.

All Kinds of Noses

Lines of ants passed each other on the sidewalk. Pairs of ants would stop and touch their feelers together. It looked very strange. Each ant was finding out where the other ant had been. They were "smelling" each other. However, insects don't have true noses. Instead, their feelers work like noses.

The main reason for noses, or feelers, is to pick up scents. All insects use their feelers, or antennae, to gather scents. A fish's nostrils do not breathe air. That would be silly. Their nostrils gather smells that help them find food.

Mammals also use their noses for breathing. Some mammals' noses have special features to help them live in their environment. A camel's nostrils close to keep out the blowing desert sand. Whales, dolphins, and beavers have nostrils that close when they swim underwater. That's a good thing! You know that getting water up your nose when you swim is an awful feeling.

Elephants have very hardworking noses. An elephant's nose is used all day to grab food, drink water, and help the elephant cool off.

SKILL PRACTICE Read the item. Write your response.

1. How do ants smell? How do you know?

_____

_____

2. Write the opinion statement in the second paragraph. How do you know it's an opinion?

_____

3. Which animals have nostrils that can close?

_____

STRATEGY PRACTICE Underline one fact and draw a box around one opinion in the second paragraph.

READ THE PASSAGE Use visualization to help you understand the information.

The Air Up There

The air surrounding Earth is the atmosphere. It is made mostly of two gases, nitrogen and the gas that we need, oxygen. Earth's gravity pulls on the gases and keeps the atmosphere close to the surface of Earth.

The atmosphere has the most gases at sea level, where the sea and land meet. As you go higher into the atmosphere, there are less gases. That means there is less oxygen to breathe. As a result, it is harder to breathe on a mountaintop than at a beach.

Outer space is where the atmosphere disappears. Astronauts who explore outer space wear special puffy suits that cover their heads and bodies. They look out of a clear window in the suit. The thick gloves are heated because space is very cold. The suits are white to reflect heat and to be seen easily against the dark background of space. Astronauts breathe oxygen from a tank on their backs. A spacesuit is a cozy atmosphere!

SKILL PRACTICE Read the item. Write your response.

1. What makes the atmosphere gases stay close to Earth's surface? Why is this important?

_____

_____

2. Where is the atmosphere thinner: 100 feet (30 m) above sea level or 2,000 feet (600 m) above sea level? How do you know?

_____

3. Name two things that are missing from outer space.

_____

STRATEGY PRACTICE Draw a picture that explains the second paragraph.

Daily Reading Comprehension • EMC 6363 • © Evan-Moor Corp.

READ THE PASSAGE Think of questions you have about the information.

What's That Hopping Down the Trail?

Is Bugs Bunny a hare or a rabbit? Hares and rabbits sure do look alike. They're both furry and have long ears and short furry tails. Their strong back legs are longer than their front legs and allow them to leap and hop. Bugs Bunny's long front teeth are typical for both hares and rabbits. These teeth are perfect for gnawing on twigs and bark, and they never stop growing. Hares and rabbits need to do a lot of chewing to keep their front teeth from growing too long.

It's hard to tell hares and rabbits apart, unless they are side by side. The hare's body is bigger and so are its ears. Its legs are longer, too. If they run a race, the hare will win. If you have one of them for a pet, it's a rabbit. Rabbits can be tamed.

The best time to tell hares and rabbits apart is when they're born. Newborn hares are covered in fur and have teeth. Their eyes are open. They are ready to run soon after they are born. Newborn rabbits do not have fur or teeth. They are deaf and blind. Both hares and rabbits can have many babies. Next time you watch Bugs on a cartoon, check him out. Is he really a rabbit?

SKILL PRACTICE Read the item. Write your response.

1. Name five ways in which rabbits and hares are alike.

_____

_____

2. Name five ways in which hares differ from rabbits.

_____

_____

3. Is Bugs Bunny a hare or a rabbit? Support your response with evidence from the text.

_____

STRATEGY PRACTICE Ask a partner a question you have about the passage.

READ THE PASSAGE Think about the information given in each paragraph.

Hardworking Insects

Honeybees and ants are easy to tell apart. Yellow and black honeybees buzz as they fly. Dark-colored ants march along the ground without a sound. Bees live in hives and ants live underground. Honeybees and ants, however, are more alike than they seem. Both kinds of insects live in communities called colonies.

Honeybees and ants build their homes. Honeybees use wax from their bodies to make six-sided cells that join to form a honeycomb. Ants dig tunnels that connect and have many rooms. Each honeybee cell and ant room has a purpose. Food is stored in some areas, and eggs hatch in others.

Every honeybee and every ant has a job to do in its colony. Some guard the home, some clean, and others care for the babies. The bees and ants that find food communicate with the others. Honeybees wiggle and dance to show the other bees where to find flowers. Ants leave a trail of scent that marks the way. The other ants follow the trail and help bring food back to the colony.

SKILL PRACTICE Read the item. Write your response.

1. What is the same about the way ants and honeybees communicate?

_____

_____

2. How is an ant's home different from a honeybee's?

_____

3. What are three things that a honeybee can do that an ant cannot?

_____

_____

STRATEGY PRACTICE Tell a partner two ways that bees and ants are the same and different.

Daily Reading Comprehension • EMC 6363 • © Evan-Moor Corp.

READ THE PASSAGE Remember as many facts as you can about banana slugs.

It's Good to Be Slimy

Banana slugs look like snails without shells. These slugs need to live in dark, damp places, where they hide under logs and leaves. They spread seeds and help plants to rot. With their yellow skin and brown spots, most banana slugs are easy to identify. Besides their bright color, banana slugs also have a hump on their backs. And they grow to an enormous size compared to other slugs. They can be ten inches (25 cm) long, which is bigger than your foot!

Banana slugs ooze slime. A thin layer covers their skin. Slime keeps the skin damp, which helps slugs breathe. The slime coating also helps protect them from injury. Like snails, slugs have one long foot, and it moves slowly. Slippery slime helps banana slugs move easily over rough rocks. The slime also gives the slug's body a texture that most animals do not like. So banana slugs have few enemies.

SKILL PRACTICE Read the item. Write your response.

1. Based on the text, what is the likely reason that banana slugs got their name?

_____

_____

2. What protects banana slugs from predators?

_____

_____

3. You are walking and spot a banana slug. Where are you and where is it?

_____

_____

STRATEGY PRACTICE Tell a partner something you want to know about banana slugs.

READ THE PASSAGE Look for clues that help you understand what is happening.

The Blue House

Tiana was not used to having neighbors. The yellow house next door had stood empty for months. The paint peeled and the stairs wobbled. Wind and rain streaked the windows with dirt. One window was cracked like a spider web. Tiana's ball had bounced over the fence and become lost in the grass.

One morning, a high-pitched noise woke Tiana. It seemed as if a swarm of giant bees were buzzing next door. Tiana peered over the fence and saw a man with a power mower. He tossed her a ball. "Is this yours?" he asked. Tiana nodded. She saw that the yellow house was no longer empty or quiet. In fact, soon it would no longer be yellow. Workers with toolboxes hurried in and out. Painters carried ladders and cans of light blue paint.

About a week later, a large van parked in front of the blue house. Workers unloaded cartons and furniture. One carried a boy's bike, too.

SKILL PRACTICE Read the item. Write your response.

1. Why was Tiana's ball lost?

_____

_____

2. Picture the van and the workers. Name four things you see them carrying into the house.

_____

3. Who is likely to be Tiana's new neighbor? How do you know?

_____

_____

STRATEGY PRACTICE Summarize the passage for a partner in four sentences or less.

READ THE PASSAGE Ask yourself questions that help you understand the information.

Giants of the Forest

Redwoods and sequoias (suh-KOY-uhz) are the tallest trees in the world. Both kinds of trees are protected by a very thick, reddish-brown bark. Both can grow to be thousands of years old and weigh over a million pounds (450,000 kg) each.

Redwoods and sequoias are found in California. Redwoods grow along the coast where there is fog. The trees take in the fog's wetness as part of their water supply. Sequoias live inland, in places where the soil is moist.

Both kinds of trees have cones. The cones contain seeds from which new trees will grow. Redwoods grow from tiny round seeds. But redwoods can also sprout from their roots or from round bumps at the base of their trunks. Often, the sprouts grow in a ring around an older tree. The circle of trees is called a fairy ring. Sequoia seeds look like thin flakes. As squirrels munch the cones, the seeds fall to the ground. The seeds have to land in good soil, not on leaves, in order to grow.

SKILL PRACTICE Read the item. Write your response.

1. Why might you see a fairy ring near a redwood tree?

_____

_____

2. Name two ways that sequoias differ from redwoods.

_____

_____

3. Name four ways in which redwoods are like sequoias.

_____

_____

STRATEGY PRACTICE Think of a question to ask a partner about the two kinds of trees.

READ THE PASSAGE   Notice how the elephant's keeper made a difference.

Big Artists

Elephants are very smart. They are social, too, and like to live in small groups. An Asian elephant named Ruby came to a zoo in Arizona. She was only a baby. Ruby had no other elephants to keep her company. Because she was bored, she got into trouble. She also liked to do something many elephants like to do. Ruby spent time holding a stick in her trunk and scribbling in the sand.

Ruby's keeper, Tawny, tried to keep Ruby busy. When Ruby was about ten years old, Tawny had an idea. What if she could teach Ruby to paint? Tawny praised Ruby and gave her treats when Ruby scribbled. Soon Tawny taught Ruby to hold a paintbrush in her trunk. Ruby seemed to enjoy it. Not long after that, Ruby began dipping the brush into buckets of colors. She painted squiggles and lines on thick paper.

Ruby soon became famous. People from all over the world came to see the painting elephant. Many people even bought Ruby's paintings!

SKILL PRACTICE   Read the item. Write your response.

1. Describe the setting of the text.

_____

_____

2. Who are the main characters? How do they interact?

_____

_____

3. What makes this elephant so unusual?

_____

STRATEGY PRACTICE   Share with a partner something you know about training a pet.

Daily Reading Comprehension • EMC 6363 • © Evan-Moor Corp.

READ THE PASSAGE   Visualize what is happening.

Moooove Out of My Way!

   A few years ago, Cinci the cow led a carefree life on a farm. Then she was sold to a company that put her in a pen. She was going to be made into meat. Before that could happen, Cinci broke free. She jumped a fence and then ran wild. Cinci zigged and zagged through the streets. She left behind a trail of torn-up lawns. Cars screeched to a halt as the cow dashed by. Cinci finally spotted a park and hid in the part of the park that had many trees. The police put food out to trap Cinci, but that plan did not work. She ate the food but still could not be caught.

   Days passed, and Cinci made the news. People everywhere cheered for the runaway cow. Ten days after Cinci had escaped, she was caught. People admired the cow who had worked so hard to be free. An artist helped raise money to save Cinci by selling many paintings. In return, he was allowed to keep Cinci. She was moved to a beautiful farm for rescued animals. When Cinci arrived, she was greeted with licks and moos from other cows. Cinci seemed to be a celebrity!

SKILL PRACTICE   Read the item. Write your response.

1. Draw two conclusions about the main character.

_____

_____

2. Why did the artist sell a lot of paintings?

_____

_____

3. What text evidence shows that people were interested in Cinci's story?

_____

STRATEGY PRACTICE   Tell a partner which part of the passage was easiest to visualize.

READ THE PASSAGE Think about what could happen.

Come! Sit! Wink!

Cocoa was a frisky puppy. He had more energy than a schoolyard full of kids. And Cocoa always did as he pleased. He ran when he was told to sit, and he dashed when he was told to stay. Mrs. Wolski, his owner, decided to take Cocoa to a school for dogs. She wanted him to learn doggy manners.

The school was a fenced-off space in a big pet store. Mrs. Wolski placed Cocoa on the floor next to a pug named Princess. Cocoa immediately nudged the pug with his elbow and winked. "Wanna go scare those cats?" he asked.

Princess shook her head and replied, "I am as perfect as my name."

"Well, how about some treats?" Cocoa pointed his paw to a shelf full of small bags. "I can rip open a bag with one bite," he boasted.

"**N-O** spells **NO**," said Princess. "I want to be the best student in the class."

Hmm…being the best sounded like a good idea to Cocoa. He sat still and listened to the teacher. He knew that Princess would be impressed!

SKILL PRACTICE Read the item. Write your response.

1. When did you first know that this story couldn't happen?

_____

_____

2. What comparison is made in the first paragraph? Why did the author do this?

_____

3. What does Princess do that a real dog wouldn't do?

_____

STRATEGY PRACTICE Tell a way that Cocoa behaves like a dog you know or have seen.

_____

Daily Reading Comprehension • EMC 6363 • © Evan-Moor Corp.

READ THE PASSAGE Visualize what is happening in the passage.

Zooktar from Jupiter

4-3-2-1 Liftoff! Sam was trying out his new computer game "Kids in Space." He watched the monitor as flames and smoke shot out from the rocket boosters. Faster than real life, the shuttle was in orbit. Sam was ready for his first adventure in space.

"Watch out, Jupiter, here I come!" said Sam. "You're the biggest planet, so you must be the best." Sam moved the astronaut, who pushed buttons and flipped switches. The shuttle neared Jupiter. Sam had to steer in and out of Jupiter's moons. His chair tilted from side to side, just like the spacecraft. Then the craft landed with a thump. Sam's chair did, too.

A figure appeared on the screen. Its voice boomed. "Hello, Sam. I'm Zooktar." Sam wondered how the game knew his name. Zooktar asked the boy a few questions. Sam's voice shook as he answered. Then Sam's mom called him for dinner. He shut down the program and looked at the game box. He saw the words in red, "WARNING: Play at your own risk. Real space travel may occur."

SKILL PRACTICE Read the item. Write your response.

1. What did Sam probably think after he read the warning on the game?

_____

_____

2. Why did Sam's voice shake as he answered the questions?

_____

3. What two facts can you learn about Jupiter from this text?

_____

STRATEGY PRACTICE Circle descriptions in the passage that helped you visualize what was fantasy.

READ THE PASSAGE Notice where the passage becomes make-believe.

What a Baby Does

Sarah smiled at Jacob, her baby brother. He lay in his crib and smiled a toothless smile back at her. Jacob was very young. Sarah wiggled a stuffed dog in front of Jacob. He kicked his skinny legs and waved his tiny arms. Sarah set the dog inside the crib. Then she leaned over and kissed the baby's head. "Good night, sleep tight," whispered Sarah. Jacob cooed in reply.

Sarah closed the door as she left. Then Jacob stood up. He swung his legs over the crib. He climbed down and reached the floor in a flash. Jacob dragged a toy chest to his window. He stood on the chest and opened the window wide. "Whoo...whoo...whoo," hooted Jacob. In moments, a barn owl silently glided into Jacob's room. The owl stood on the floor while Jacob sat. The baby snatched a deck of cards from under the owl's wings. "It's my turn to deal," said Jacob.

SKILL PRACTICE Read the item. Write your response.

1. Why did the writer have the passage take place in the baby's bedroom?

_____

_____

2. List two clues from the first paragraph that point toward Jacob being a few months old.

_____

3. Write the sentence that first let you know that this is a fantasy. How did you know?

_____

STRATEGY PRACTICE Which character in the passage would you want to be? Why?

_____

_____

READ THE PASSAGE Think about why the author wrote the passage.

Junk in Space

Outer space is crowded with trash. You won't find banana peels and plastic bags. But there are pieces of booster rockets, paint chips, and bolts. Most of the trash is small. About 200,000 pieces are very small. But small pieces cause problems. Each piece of trash travels at a high speed. When two pieces crash, they explode. They create hundreds of pieces. More pieces means more problems.

Space is crowded with large items, too. Scientists sometimes can prevent large things from crashing. In 2008, they moved the International Space Station several miles. This stopped the station from hitting a tank of gas. But it is not easy to control all the stuff in space. In February 2009, two satellites were traveling at a speed of 25,000 miles per hour (40,000 km per hour). They hit each other. As a result, they created a huge cloud of dust and a lot of trash.

Scientists know how to launch things into space. Now they need to figure out how to clean up the mess.

SKILL PRACTICE Read the item. Write your response.

1. Why did the author write this text? How do you know?

_____

2. What happens when objects in space run into each other?

_____

3. What does the author want scientists to do? State the text evidence.

_____

_____

STRATEGY PRACTICE Write a question you have about information from the passage.

_____

READ THE PASSAGE Pay attention to each numbered step.

What's Hiding?

Animals have a way of hiding in plain sight. Their skin or fur blends into their environment. This form of camouflage helps them survive.

You can make a peephole drawing and challenge a friend to identify a camouflaged animal. You will need two sheets of plain white paper, a pencil, markers or crayons, scissors, and a stapler.

First, look in a book or on the Internet for an animal that blends into its habitat. Then follow these steps:

1. Draw and color a large picture of the animal on one sheet of white paper.
2. Cut a peephole in the other sheet of paper. Make sure part of the animal will show through that hole.
3. Staple the peephole page to the animal drawing along the very top.
4. Draw and color the animal's habitat on the top page. Make sure your drawing blends with the part of the animal that shows through the peephole.
5. Let the guessing begin! Give a clue, if you wish.

SKILL PRACTICE Read the item. Write your response.

1. Why did the author write this text? How do you know?

_____

2. Why is the reader told to find out about a camouflaged animal before beginning?

_____

_____

3. Why might this project be difficult to do?

_____

_____

STRATEGY PRACTICE Tell a partner about another project or craft you have done recently.

READ THE PASSAGE   Think about what Fox and Snail will do next.

A Forest Tale

There once was a forest full of animals. Some nested in the trees. Others slithered among the fallen leaves. Many hopped, while others strolled. Among the animals, there was one red fox. That fox was speedy. Fox bragged, "Absolutely no one is faster than me!"

Fox liked to challenge animals to race. After all, winning was easy for him. He ran hard no matter who his opponent was. Fox whooshed past the snake, and he zipped past the squirrel. He zoomed past the quick brown hare. Fox beat every single forest animal except the one who did not care to race. That was Snail. She was never in a hurry. She carried a heavy shell on her back. And she had only one foot. That foot got Snail everywhere she wanted to go. But in a race, four feet are usually better than one.

One day, Snail was tired of hearing Fox boast about his speed. "I will race you, Fox," announced Snail.

SKILL PRACTICE   Read the item. Write your response.

1. What do you think will happen next?

_____

_____

2. If Fox wins the race, what will he most likely say to Snail?

_____

3. Describe Fox's personality. Use a piece of text evidence.

_____

STRATEGY PRACTICE   Write a question that helped you get more involved in the story.

_____

READ THE PASSAGE Use clues from the passage to figure out what will happen next.

Hoover, Our Vacuum Cleaner

Our puppy Hoover loves to eat. She pretends to be choosy. If you offer her a treat, Hoover will first sniff it. Then, Hoover gobbles the treat in one bite. Hoover will eat almost anything that's outdoors. She chews grass and flowers. And she catches flying bugs with a fast chomp. We once caught her gnawing a garden hose! Hoover likes to eat what we're eating, too. She whimpers when we eat ears of corn. I give her the ear when I'm done with it. She stretches out on the floor and holds the ear with her front paws. Then she munches away.

Hoover walks with her nose sniffing the floor. She eats nearly anything she finds. One night, she pried open the pantry door. Hoover knocked down a box and chewed it open. Dad found Hoover sitting in a pile of cereal.

Hoover's favorite room in the house is the kitchen. She likes sitting under the baby's highchair. The baby is learning how to eat. Often, the baby drops his food.

SKILL PRACTICE Read the item. Write your response.

1. Why does Hoover's name fit her?

_____

_____

2. What would happen if someone left her purse with a granola bar in it sitting on the floor?

_____

_____

3. Which sentence tells you why Hoover sits under the baby's highchair? Explain.

_____

STRATEGY PRACTICE Think about a dog you know or have seen. Tell a partner how Hoover is or is <u>not</u> like that dog.

READ THE PASSAGE Think about why the author wrote the passage.

Mail Mules

Some mules work for the United States Post Office. They deliver the mail to a small village at the bottom of the Grand Canyon. A tribe of Native Americans lives there. The only way to reach them is by a dirt path. That path twists and turns down and down for thousands of feet. The path is too narrow and dangerous for trucks. The wind is too fierce for helicopters. One mail carrier and a team of mules are brave enough to make the trip. They carefully clop downhill 8 miles (13 km). After 3 hours, they reach the bottom of the canyon. They deliver the goods and return to the canyon's rim. That hike takes another 3 hours. They do this every day, even in rain, snow, or the blazing sun.

The Native Americans live 120 miles (190 km) from the nearest store. The mules bring them everything they need. The mules deliver mail, milk, and medicine. They also bring furniture and frozen foods. The supplies are unloaded and left at the post office. The people go there to pick up their orders.

SKILL PRACTICE Read the item. Write your response.

1. Why did the author write this text?

_____

_____

2. What would the tribe do if there was no mail delivery?

_____

_____

3. The author wants to lengthen the text. What part should he or she tell more about?

_____

STRATEGY PRACTICE Share a question you have about the information in the passage.

READ THE PASSAGE   Look for the most important information.

What a Catch!

People crowded in front of the huge tank of fish. They pointed to the gray fish with the white belly. It was a great white shark! A diver was feeding the shark. The year was 2004. The shark was a new exhibit at an aquarium. It was the first great white shark to eat in front of people. The shark lived in the tank with sea turtles, tuna, and other kinds of sharks. Six months went by, and about one million people came to see the shark. Then the great white began to hunt the other sharks. The aquarium released the great white shark into the ocean.

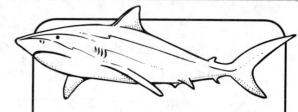

Great White Shark Facts

- swim up to 25 miles per hour (40 km per hour)
- can go three months without eating
- have 2 to 14 babies at one time
- have a powerful sense of smell
- are endangered

SKILL PRACTICE   Read the item. Write your response.

1. Why did the author use bullets in the sidebar?

_____

_____

2. Why did a million people visit the great white shark exhibit?

_____

_____

3. Why did the aquarium let the great white shark go?

_____

STRATEGY PRACTICE   Underline the sentence in the passage that explains why the shark in the aquarium was special.

READ THE TABLE OF CONTENTS Study the table of contents, and then use it to answer the questions.

Table of Contents

SKILL PRACTICE Read the item. Write your response.

1. How are the stories organized in this book? How do you know?

_____

_____

2. You see an illustration on page 23. What is the title of its story?

_____

3. In what chapter and on what page does "What a Skunk Needs to Do" start?

_____

STRATEGY PRACTICE Why is the front of a book a good place for a table of contents?

READ THE ADVERTISEMENT   Focus on the most important information.

Just What You Need for School!

A16

Blue or red. Good in all kinds of weather. Holds up to 25 pounds (11 kg). Outside pockets. Padded shoulder straps.

A17

Black or tan. Large pouch with button. Padded shoulder straps. Holds up to 6 pounds (2.7 kg).

A18

Gray. Good in all kinds of weather. Two zippered pockets. Wide shoulder straps. Holds up to 10 pounds (4.5 kg).

SKILL PRACTICE   Read the item. Write your response.

1. What is the purpose of this text? What is it missing?

_____

_____

2. Why might model A18 be less comfortable than the other backpacks?

_____

_____

3. Which backpack would you choose? Tell why you picked that one.

_____

_____

STRATEGY PRACTICE   Circle the information in the advertisement that you think is most important to know when you buy a backpack.

Notice what information is given in the selection.

Toys Through Time

Long ago, children made their own toys. They used whatever they could find, such as boxes, yarn, and paper. Their toys were simple. Today, toys are bought in stores. Many are electronic and are operated by small computers. These toys have parts that light up, talk, or move.

The timeline below shows when some popular toys were invented.

Dollhouse	Teddy bear	Slinky®	Game Boy®	Leapster®
Roller skates	Crayons	Tonka® trucks	Action figures	Xbox®
Jigsaw puzzle	Mickey Mouse®	Candy Land®	Tickle Me Elmo®	Wii®
Talking doll	Stuffed toy	Mr. Potato Head®	Beanie Babies®	Guitar Hero®
Toy train	Monopoly®	LEGO®	Furby®	
1700s–1900	**1900s–1930s**	**1940s–1960s**	**1970s–2000**	**2000–Today**

SKILL PRACTICE Read the item. Write your response.

1. List three toys that children played with during the 1960s.

_____

_____

2. Your uncle was born in 1980. Name two toys that were popular when he was your age.

_____

_____

3. Find a toy or game you enjoy and tell when it first appeared according to the timeline.

_____

STRATEGY PRACTICE Discuss the kinds of information the timeline presents.

READ THE PASSAGE   Decide which details are the most important.

Life in an Ant Colony

This diagram shows a small part of an ant colony. Thousands of ants often live together. Groups of ants do different jobs to help the colony. For example, some ants guard the home. They know who to keep out because every ant in the colony has the same smell. Outsiders smell different.

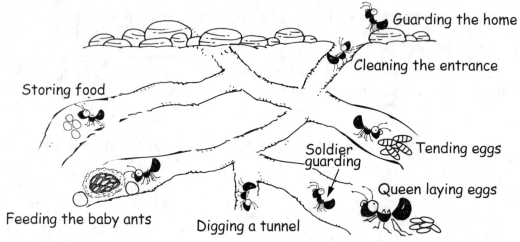

Guarding the home

Cleaning the entrance

Storing food

Tending eggs

Soldier guarding

Queen laying eggs

Feeding the baby ants

Digging a tunnel

SKILL PRACTICE   Read the item. Write your response.

1. How do the labels support the diagram?

_____

2. How do guard ants protect the entrances?

_____

_____

3. How could this diagram be improved?

_____

STRATEGY PRACTICE   Write a sentence that tells an important idea of the passage.

_____

READ THE PASSAGE Stop after each paragraph and ask yourself what it was about.

When Ramona Quimby first appeared in 1955, she was four years old. She turned nine in 1989. Ramona is the main character in a series of books written by Beverly Cleary. For many years, kids have laughed at Ramona's adventures. After all, Ramona once wore her soft blue pajamas under her school clothes. And she tried to dye herself blue.

Beverly Cleary grew up in Portland, Oregon. Her family lived near Klickitat Street. It became the name of the street where Ramona lives.

Kids all over the world know about Ramona Quimby. The books can be read in 14 languages. Videos and television programs have been made from the stories. Statues of Ramona, her friend Henry Huggins, and his dog Ribsy are in a park close to Klickitat Street. Kids can splash in the fountains of water under the feet of the statues. If Ramona were real, she'd join right in!

SKILL PRACTICE Read the item. Write your response.

1. Is Ramona a real person? How do you know?

_____

_____

2. Write one detail from the text about Ramona.

_____

3. What would be a good title for this text?

_____

STRATEGY PRACTICE What advice would you give someone who could not stay focused while reading the passage?

_____

_____

READ THE PASSAGE Notice the main idea and important facts about it.

Prickly Desert Plants

Plants need the right amounts of sun and water to survive. Desert plants get plenty of sun but not much water. Rain might not fall for months. And when rain does fall, it evaporates quickly. Desert plants must use water carefully in order to live in the hot, dry desert.

Many types of cactuses live in the desert. Most have prickly spines that are a type of leaf. Some spines are short and cover the plant. They shade the cactus from the hot sun. Some cactuses have long spines. These catch rain and direct it down the stem to the roots.

Cactus roots are not deep, but they stretch far away from the plant. Cactus roots grow when it rains. Then the plant can absorb more water. A cactus stores the rain inside the stem, where it cannot evaporate. Its thick skin expands to hold the water.

A cactus stores water and uses it slowly. People can learn about careful water use from a cactus!

SKILL PRACTICE Read the item. Write your response.

1. What is the second paragraph about?

_____

2. What is the main idea of the third paragraph?

_____

3. How does the last paragraph relate to the first paragraph?

_____

_____

STRATEGY PRACTICE In your own words, tell a partner four important details that you read in the passage.

READ THE PASSAGE   Notice the steps Jake takes to get ready to bat.

Jake Is Up to Bat

"Let's go, Tigers!" The fans clap their hands as they cheer. Jake sits in the team's dugout. He has been playing baseball since he was five. Now that he's nine, he's a good player. He stays focused and calm even when the score is close. He watches the game carefully from the dugout.

When it's Jake's turn to bat, he has a method for getting ready. He first grabs his favorite bat. He swings it twice to loosen up. Then, he steps confidently into the batter's box. Jake puts down the bat and leans it against his legs. Then, he hikes up his pants and tugs on both of his batter's gloves.

With his uniform just right, Jake takes hold of the bat. He taps the tip into the dirt three times. Next, he stares at the pitcher and takes two more practice swings. All the while, he's thinking about hitting the ball. He doesn't even hear the crowd yell to get a hit. Jake plants his feet firmly in place. He nods his head. He's now ready for the first pitch.

SKILL PRACTICE   Read the item. Write your response.

1. What are the first two actions that Jake takes when it's his turn at bat?

_____

2. What does Jake do right after he stares at the pitcher?

_____

_____

3. How long has Jake been playing baseball? How do you know?

_____

_____

STRATEGY PRACTICE   With a partner, act out the steps Jake takes to get ready to bat. Make sure you do the steps in the same order as Jake.

READ THE PASSAGE Remember the steps for making pizza dough.

Twirling Dough

My family and I go to Uncle Gino's house for dinner on the last Saturday of every month. That's when he makes pizza twirl.

Before we arrive, Uncle Gino shapes the pizza dough into a ball. After we get there, my job is to spread flour on his work space. Then I sit on a kitchen stool and watch the pizza expert at work. Uncle Gino removes his watch and ring. Next, he dusts the ball of dough with flour. Then he uses his fingers to press down on the dough. He presses over and over as he shapes the dough into a flat circle. Uncle Gino says that a ten-inch (25-cm) circle is best for tossing.

My favorite part comes next. Uncle Gino closes his hands into fists. He carefully drapes the circle of dough over his hands. I say, "Get ready, get set, toss!" Uncle Gino flings the dough into the air with a spin. It twirls around before he catches it on the backs of his fists. Then he tosses it again. The dough stretches bigger each time he catches it.

SKILL PRACTICE Read the item. Write your response.

1. When does Uncle Gino remove his watch and ring? Why does he do it?

_____

_____

2. What is the narrator's favorite part?

_____

_____

3. What does the narrator do to help Uncle Gino?

_____

STRATEGY PRACTICE Look back at the passage. Circle the important steps that Uncle Gino follows for tossing pizza dough.

READ THE PASSAGE   Think of questions you have about the information.

From the Mouth to the Body

Some parts of your body work together like a team to do important jobs. These teams are called systems. Your digestive system is made up of your body parts that work together to break down your food.

The job of breaking down food begins with your mouth. Your teeth break up the food you eat into a size you can swallow.

Swallowing sends the food down your throat. Your throat connects to a tube called the esophagus (ih-SOF-uh-gus). Muscles in the esophagus squeeze together and push the food down into your stomach. The stomach walls move in and out. This causes the food to mix and churn. It becomes like a thick soup. The soupy food is then squeezed into the small intestine.

The food is still too big for your body to use. So fluids enter the intestine and break down the food more. Then the food is small enough to enter your bloodstream. The blood delivers the food to the cells in your body.

SKILL PRACTICE   Read the item. Write your response.

1. What is the main idea of this text?

_____

_____

2. Where and how in the human body does food first begin to break down?

_____

3. Where are pieces of food small enough to enter the bloodstream? Explain how.

_____

_____

STRATEGY PRACTICE   In your own words, tell a partner the main idea of the passage.

READ THE PASSAGE Look for reasons why things happen.

Not the Way to Start the Day

Sophie rushed as she got ready for school. She had waited until last night to do her book report. Sophie's idea was great. She had created a small stage and finger puppets to retell the story she had read. But Sophie spent most of the night putting it all together. She did the rest of her homework that morning.

The stage and puppets were in the car and so was Sophie's mom. She did not want to be late for work. Sophie's mom blasted the horn. The noise startled Sneakers, Sophie's cat. He dashed in front of Sophie just as she started to zip her backpack. Sophie tripped and out flew her papers. Gonzo woke up, ready for a chase. As the dog ran, his claws pierced Sophie's homework. Now it was full of tiny holes. Sneakers jumped onto the table, where he thought he was safe. Gonzo stood on his hind legs and plopped his big paws near the cat. As he barked, one paw knocked over a glass of juice. Sophie saw the juice drip slowly and steadily onto her homework. She would have a lot of explaining to do at school!

SKILL PRACTICE Read the item. Write your response.

1. How does the car horn start a chain reaction?

_____

_____

2. Why didn't Sophie finish her homework the night before?

_____

_____

3. What is Sophie going to have to explain at school? Who will ask for the explanation?

_____

STRATEGY PRACTICE Underline verbs in the passage that helped you visualize the actions.

READ THE PASSAGE   Notice the causes of things that happen.

Please Make Spelling Simple

Do you have trouble spelling? Do you think that the rules are confusing? If you do, most people would agree with you. In fact, about 100 years ago, Andrew Carnegie tried to make changes in the English language. He correctly predicted that English would become the most important language in the world. So he wanted to make English easier to read and write. He gathered together a group of 30 very smart men. They created new spellings for 300 common words.

The men believed that words should be spelled the way they sound. So they used the letters for the sounds they heard and got rid of silent letters. For example, *surprise* was spelled *surprize, ghost* became *gost,* and *through* became *thru.*

Most of the spelling changes that the men suggested never happened. But, thanks to Andrew Carnegie, we now write *fantasy* instead of *phantasy* and *hiccup* instead of *hiccough.*

SKILL PRACTICE   Read the item. Write your response.

1. Why did Carnegie want to make English easier to read and write?

_____

_____

2. Why were silent letters eliminated in the new spellings? State text evidence.

_____

_____

3. Why do you think that most of the spelling changes the men suggested didn't happen?

_____

STRATEGY PRACTICE   Look at the second paragraph. Circle the sentence that tells a cause. Underline the sentence that describes the effect.

READ THE PASSAGE Look for words that give someone's opinion.

Up, Up, and Away!

"Impossible!" said some. "It's foolish!" said others. Frenchman Jean-Pierre Blanchard claimed that he could fly. He had come to America with his hot-air balloon. President George Washington thought the idea was wonderful and wished Blanchard good luck. Scientists asked to go along on the flight. But Blanchard said no. He wanted the honor all to himself. As he was ready to lift off, however, something furry was shoved into his hands. A small dog would share Blanchard's fame!

Cannons fired and bands played. The balloon rose slowly into the sky. Blanchard waved his feathered hat and a small flag to the crowds below. They cheered from roads, fields, and even rooftops. Blanchard liked all of the attention.

The balloon sailed over a river. It seemed as narrow as a ribbon to Blanchard. Thin clouds looked like pulled cotton. About 46 minutes later, Blanchard landed the balloon in a farmer's field. He and the dog had flown 15 miles (24 km). The farmer had never seen a man come down from the clouds. He ran off into the woods!

SKILL PRACTICE Read the item. Write your response.

1. Which fact let you know that this balloon flight happened long ago?

_____

_____

2. Write the sentence that is an opinion in paragraph two. How do you know?

_____

3. What caused the farmer to run into the woods?

_____

STRATEGY PRACTICE Describe to a partner a scene in the passage that you most enjoyed visualizing.

READ THE PASSAGE Notice what is fact and what is opinion.

Filming Animals

Some marine animals and land animals make movies. They actually do the filming! Cameras called Crittercams are safely and gently attached to the animals. The cameras record pictures and sounds for scientists to study. Scientists believe that the cameras are the best tools for studying animals in the wild. Best of all, the animals aren't bothered by the cameras.

Marine animals were the first Crittercam moviemakers. In 1989, a sea turtle had a Crittercam strapped to its back. The camera soon fell off. Four years later, cameras were attached to seals, using safe, sticky patches. In 1996, special suction cups were used to attach cameras to whales. In 1999, penguins wore backpacks.

Scientists thought it was important to try cameras on land animals. In 2003, a Crittercam sat on the back of a lion hunting in Africa. Today, bears, lions, and hyenas wear the cameras as collars. Crittercam gives us an up-close look at the secret lives of wild animals. These films are exciting to watch!

SKILL PRACTICE Read the item. Write your response.

1. Write two opinion statements from the text. How do you know they are opinions?

_____

_____

2. Why are the facts in the first paragraph essential to the text?

_____

3. Why do you think the scientists used Crittercams on marine animals first?

_____

STRATEGY PRACTICE Which paragraph gives the most information chronologically?

_____

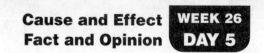

READ THE PASSAGE   Visualize the animal as you read.

Hanging Around

Sloths are animals that make their homes in trees. This flat-faced mammal lives in rainforests. It spends most of its time hanging from tree branches. A sloth is adapted to live its life hanging like a hammock.

A tree is a place of safety for a sloth, and the ground is not. Long, curved claws on each foot help it climb a tree and hang. With strong shoulder and neck muscles, a sloth can hang with ease. But a sloth's back legs are so weak, it cannot stand. It is a plant eater, so food is handy in a tree. A sloth simply tugs on a branch until its long tongue can reach the leaves.

Spotting a sloth is not easy. For one thing, it stays very still and moves ever so slowly. It may take the mammal a day to inch from one tree to another. And all of the moisture in the rainforest causes tiny green algae to grow on the sloth's brown fur. With a mossy-green color, the sloth blends right in with its home. Going "green" is easy for a sloth!

SKILL PRACTICE   Read the item. Write your response.

1. What causes a sloth's fur to be a mossy-green color?

_____

_____

2. What is the effect of the sloth's strong neck and shoulder muscles?

_____

3. Jenny says, "This scooter is as speedy as a sloth!" What does she mean?

_____

_____

STRATEGY PRACTICE   Describe a sloth, using details you visualized as you read.

READ THE PASSAGE Find ways that you and trees are the same and different.

Trees and You

You're not covered in bark, and birds don't nest in your hair. Unlike a tree, you can't be made into furniture and paper. And yet you and a tree are alike in some ways.

First of all, you both are living things. Like you, trees need water, air, and food to survive. Trees make their own food by using water, air, and energy from the sun. Your body takes the food and water you give it and changes them into the nutrients it needs.

Parts of your body and parts of a tree have the same names. The top of a tree is called the crown, which is another name for your head. The main part of both your body and a tree is called a trunk. The arms and legs that extend from your trunk are called limbs. Another name for a tree's branches is limbs.

You and a tree have parts that do similar jobs. Like a tree's outer covering of bark, your skin protects your insides. Tubes in a tree carry water and nutrients throughout the tree. Your blood vessels work in much the same way.

SKILL PRACTICE Read the item. Write your response.

1. Write three ways in which people and trees are alike.

_____

_____

2. Write three ways in which trees differ from people.

_____

_____

3. Which part of a tree is used for a telephone pole? How do you know?

_____

STRATEGY PRACTICE Ask a partner a question that can be answered by the passage.

Stop after each paragraph and recall what you read.

A Way to Compare Trees

All trees have green leaves. Leaves soak up sunlight and use that energy to make food for the tree. Most trees can be divided into two groups based on their leaves.

Broadleaf trees have flat leaves. Most broadleaf trees turn red, orange, or yellow every autumn and then lose all of their leaves. Many of these trees have flowers that grow into fruit. The fruit contains the seeds that will grow into more trees. Many broadleaf trees have very hard wood, so they are called hardwoods. Their wood is used to make furniture, baseball bats, and hockey sticks.

Needleleaf trees have narrow leaves that grow close together. Most needleleaf trees are called evergreens because they stay green all year round. Old needles turn brown and fall off. But the young green needles remain on the tree. Most evergreens grow cones that hold the trees' seeds. Evergreens are known as softwoods. Paper and building lumber are made from softwood trees.

SKILL PRACTICE Read the item. Write your response.

1. Write three ways in which broadleaf and needleleaf trees are different.

_____

_____

2. Write two ways in which broadleaf and needleleaf trees are alike.

_____

_____

3. Which type of tree is a cherry tree? How do you know?

_____

STRATEGY PRACTICE Underline some of the words and phrases that helped you visualize how broadleaf and needleleaf trees are alike and different.

Daily Reading Comprehension • EMC 6363 • © Evan-Moor Corp.

READ THE PASSAGE Remember the important facts about the pets you read about.

Presidential Pets

1600 Pennsylvania Avenue is a world-famous address. It is the address of the White House, where the president of the United States lives and works. Animals of all sorts have lived in the White House along with their famous owners. It has been the home of a snake named Emily Spinach, a badger called Josiah, and Billy the hippo.

Dogs have been a popular White House pet through the years. Charlie, King Tut, and Miss Beazley were pet pooches. Yuki and her presidential owner liked to howl together in his office. Another president saved a chair at important meetings for his dog Laddie Boy. A pooch called Liberty was allowed to say goodbye to special guests. Two dogs, Millie and Buddy, have books written about them.

Some presidents kept practical animals. Pauline the cow provided milk. A flock of sheep once mowed the lawns. Other animals were more unusual. Alligators, a wallaby, and a bobcat named Smokey have lived at the White House. Macaroni the pony once grazed on the lawns but not when the coyote and zebra stayed there.

SKILL PRACTICE Read the item. Write your response.

1. When were Pauline and the sheep probably kept?

_____

_____

2. What conclusion can you draw about the presidents in this text?

_____

3. Have all the animals at the White House been tame? How do you know?

_____

STRATEGY PRACTICE Write a question that you asked yourself as you read the passage.

_____

READ THE PASSAGE   Find out what famous face is being written about.

A Face People Know

About 50 years ago, Harvey Ball was asked to make a drawing for a company. The company wanted its workers to be friendly and happy. Mr. Ball took a thin black marker and drew a circle on yellow paper. Inside the circle, he drew two small black ovals. Then he added a big, curved smile. Within minutes, he had created the smiley face. His smiley face drawing was made into 100 buttons. Soon, 10,000 more buttons were ordered.

A few years later, two brothers named Spain drew a smiley face. They added the words, "Have a nice day." Millions and millions of their smiley face buttons were sold. And smiley faces appeared on all kinds of products, including stuffed smiley dolls.

Mr. Ball believed that a smiling face was important. In 1999, he began the first "World Smile Day." He has brought a lot of smiles to the world.

SKILL PRACTICE   Read the item. Write your response.

1. Why were 10,000 smiley face buttons ordered?

_____

_____

2. Draw two conclusions about yellow smiley faces.

_____

_____

3. Use text evidence to tell why Harvey Ball started World Smile Day.

_____

_____

STRATEGY PRACTICE   Discuss with a partner where you have seen this famous face.

READ THE PASSAGE Remember how the kinds of grasses are alike and different.

Grasses That People Eat

Rice, corn, and wheat are called cereal grasses because they are grown mostly as food. Rice, corn, and wheat are grown in different ways, but their grains, or seeds, are a rich source of food.

Rice grows in fields called paddies that are flooded with water. Rice is the most important food for many people in the world. Its stems, called straw, are used to make rugs and roofs.

Corn is planted in rows in large fields. Farmers pump water between the rows. One stalk of corn can grow to 15 feet (4.5 m) high. It holds between one and four ears of corn. The seeds, or kernels, on each ear are made into cornflakes and corn chips, or eaten as corn niblets. Corn is also used to make fuel, crayons, and dyes.

Wheat was one of the first grasses grown by people. It does not need a lot of water to grow. Wheat is used to make spaghetti and cereal. Wheat flour is used in baked goods. The stems make a good straw, used as bedding for animals.

SKILL PRACTICE Read the item. Write your response.

1. Name a fact about rice and corn that does not apply to wheat.

_____

_____

2. Draw two conclusions from the text.

_____

_____

3. Which cereal grass do you like best? Explain.

_____

STRATEGY PRACTICE Have a partner ask you a question about the passage. Then answer it.

READ THE PASSAGE Think about where otters live and how they behave.

Looking Good!

You spend time each day washing up and brushing your hair and teeth. You do this to stay healthy. Sea otters spend hours each day grooming themselves. They have to. Grooming keeps sea otters alive.

Sea otters have the thickest fur of all animals. Their plush coat holds air bubbles. The air bubbles work like a shield against the cold Pacific Ocean where sea otters live. If the cold water reaches a sea otter's skin, the animal can freeze to death. Using their front paws, sea otters press water out of their fur. Air bubbles move in to replace the water. Sea otters also blow into their fur to trap air.

Matted, messy, or dirty fur cannot hold air bubbles. Food and kelp can get onto sea otters' fur. They use their sharp claws like combs to clean and untangle their fur. They roll and twist and bend in a complete circle to get to every bit of mess. Their fur is loose. So, if they can't quite reach a part, they simply pull it closer.

SKILL PRACTICE Read the item. Write your response.

1. Where do sea otters live?

_____

2. How does grooming help sea otters survive?

_____

3. What do sea otters do if food or kelp gets tangled in their fur? Why?

_____

_____

STRATEGY PRACTICE Write one way otters and people are similar and one way they are different.

_____

READ THE PASSAGE Visualize the passage and the ways Peter reacts to his aunt.

My Name Is Peter!

Peter hid behind the living room curtain. Every few moments, he pulled back a bit of the cloth to peek outside. Soon the truck would pull up. Aunt Mitzi never missed his birthday. Peter dreaded her arrival. He knew what would happen.

A red truck pulled up to the curb with its horn beeping. The whole neighborhood would know Aunt Mitzi had arrived. Peter froze as he watched his aunt stride up the driveway. There was no getting away. He turned to the door as Aunt Mitzi rushed in.

"Petey!" she boomed. Peter's face turned red. Aunt Mitzi hugged Peter so tightly that she lifted him off the floor. Then she landed a red-lipstick kiss right on his cheek.

"Uh, hi, Aunt Mitzi," Peter grunted.

Aunt Mitzi smiled at Peter all afternoon, and she pinched his cheeks, too. "You've gotten so big, Petey!" she marveled. Peter didn't mind the big hug, and he actually liked the attention. But he hated the nickname.

SKILL PRACTICE Read the item. Write your response.

1. Describe the setting.

_____

_____

2. Use text evidence to tell how Peter could be so certain his Aunt Mitzi would come.

_____

3. What does Aunt Mitzi do that causes Peter to blush?

_____

STRATEGY PRACTICE Underline verbs in the passage that helped you visualize what you read.

READ THE PASSAGE Think about what can and cannot happen.

Why Bears Have Short Tails

Long before you were born, Bear had a long, thick tail. It swished as Bear walked. Animals remarked that Bear had the finest tail in the forest. This talk made Fox gnash his teeth. He plotted how to make his red, bushy tail the grandest.

Although it was a very cold winter, the stream was still flowing. Fox caught some fish and trotted off to find Bear. The fish made Bear's stomach growl with hunger. Fox claimed that he had caught the fish in the frozen lake. Bear could do the same, Fox said. All Bear had to do was cut a hole in the ice. Then he was to drop his tail into the hole and sit on the ice until sunset. At nightfall, Bear should jump up quickly. His tail would be full of fish.

Bear did exactly as Fox had suggested. Bear's tail tingled while he sat in the cold. As night fell, Bear tried to stand. His tail stuck to the ice. He tugged with all his strength. At last, he jumped up. Bear turned his head to look back at his dinner. He expected to see a tail full of fish, but all he saw was a short stump.

From that day to this day, every bear has a short, stubby tail.

SKILL PRACTICE Read the item. Write your response.

1. Where would you be likely to read this text? Explain.

_____

_____

2. How do you know that this story didn't really happen?

_____

3. What happened to Bear's long, thick tail?

_____

STRATEGY PRACTICE Share how you determined what was real and what was fantasy in the passage.

READ THE PASSAGE   Notice where you first realize that the passage is fantasy.

No Pet? No Problem!

Hannah decided that she was old enough to have a pet. Her dad had a different idea. He offered to buy Hannah a plant. He explained that a plant needed some of the same kind of care as an animal. If Hannah took good care of the plant, she would prove she was ready for a pet. "No problem," said Hannah.

Hannah and her dad drove to a plant nursery. Hannah chose a violet with fuzzy leaves and bright purple flowers. A florist told Hannah that a violet needed light, water, and food. "No problem," said Hannah.

Hannah cleared a space on her floor for her violet. She filled a glass with water and added a straw. "Here you go," said Hannah, and she watched the plant slurp. She offered the plant a spoonful of food and said, "Open wide." Hannah then plugged in a lamp and handed the switch to the violet. "Turn this on when I'm at school," she ordered.

Time passed, and the violet grew strong and healthy. Hannah decided to ask her dad for a kitten. She figured that this time her dad would say, "No problem."

SKILL PRACTICE   Read the item. Write your response.

1. Why did Hannah's dad say she had to take care of a plant?

_____

_____

2. Which of Hannah's actions could not really happen?

_____

3. What will Hannah's dad probably say when she asks for a pet now? Explain.

_____

STRATEGY PRACTICE   Write three words or phrases from the passage that you visualized.

READ THE PASSAGE   Think about what can and cannot happen.

The Royal Family

Wendy and Mike sat on the warm sand as waves licked the beach. The kids scooped, flattened, and piled the sand. Hours later, a castle with towers and walls stood proudly. The kids finished as the sun seemed to slip into the sea.

Three hermit crabs peeked from behind a rock. The largest crab waved at the others to follow him. They paraded to the castle to check it out. Papa Crab kicked the castle with a claw. "It's a well-constructed home," he concluded.

"But all this brown is so dull!" complained Mama Crab.

"It just needs some kelp on the walls," suggested Baby Crab. He was already in the castle, looking for a dungeon to play in.

"Then let's move in!" Mama Crab shouted. "Right on!" said Papa Crab. Mama and Papa Crab gave a high-five with their antennas.

The hermit crabs became the royal family of the beach.

SKILL PRACTICE   Read the item. Write your response.

1. Who created the sand castle? How do you know?

_____

_____

2. What is the first detail in the text that let you know it was a fantasy?

_____

_____

3. At what time of day do the hermit crabs come to check out the sand castle?

_____

_____

STRATEGY PRACTICE   Tell a partner about two connections you made to the passage.

READ THE PASSAGE   Think about what the author wants you to know.

Flip and Catch!

Native Americans who lived in wooded areas liked to play a game. They flipped and caught bone disks in a wooden bowl. The Native Americans gathered twigs to use as counters. You need just a few things to play this game. Play it once as described below. Then make up a new version.

To prepare: Get a container with a flat bottom. Then, cut six circles about four inches (10 cm) across out of heavy paper. Make a design on one side of each circle. The designs that you create do not have to be the same. Finally, get 48 toothpicks.

To play: A player puts the circles into the container and flips the circles into the air. The player tries to catch the circles in the container.

To score: If a circle lands in the container with the design side up, the player gets one toothpick. If the circle lands blank side up, the player doesn't get a toothpick. Subtract one toothpick for every circle that lands outside of the container. Play the game until all 48 toothpicks are used. The player with the most toothpicks wins.

SKILL PRACTICE   Read the item. Write your response.

1. Why did the author write this text?

_____

_____

2. What is the purpose of the first paragraph?

_____

_____

3. Does this sound like something you'd like to do? Tell why or why not.

_____

STRATEGY PRACTICE   What is the author's purpose in the second paragraph?

_____

READ THE PASSAGE   Think about what the author wants you to know.

They're Everywhere!

Tiny specks float all over the world. People try to get rid of them, but they can't make them disappear. You can write your name in the specks, and they can make you sneeze. The specks are dust.

Everything in the universe breaks down into dust. Even space is filled with dust. When objects crash, they blow up into dust. Stars explode into dust. Comets form from dust and ice. The astronauts stirred up layers of dust on the moon. Meteorites that crash on the moon's surface create dust. The robots sent to Mars landed on rusty-orange dust. There are no plants to keep the dust in place, so strong storms can cover the planet in dust.

Everything on Earth is always crumbling into dust. Plants and trees rot, and the bits get blown around. Shoes kick up soil, and volcanoes cough out ash. Pencil shavings, hair strands, and bits of paper form some of the dust that's in your classroom. Even your body creates dust. Your body makes new skin cells every day. The old cells flake off as dead skin, or dust.

SKILL PRACTICE   Read the item. Write your response.

1. Why did the author write this text?

_____

2. What did the author do to prepare to write the text?

_____

_____

3. Can we ever be free of dust? Explain why or why not.

_____

STRATEGY PRACTICE   Underline a sentence that shows the author trying to make a connection with you.

READ THE PASSAGE Think about what may happen next.

How Do You Trick a Cat?

Mazy does not like her cat carrier. She has to get into it every time she goes to the vet. Mazy does not care that the carrier is soft and pink. The white bows and brown polka dots do not impress Mazy at all. When she sees the carrier, she speeds away faster than a race car. And like all smart cats, Mazy knows where to hide so she can't be found.

Luiz is nervous. He needs to take Mazy to the vet for shots. He has to get to the vet's office on time. And most of all, he must have a good plan to get Mazy into the carrier without any trouble. Only a trick will do.

Luiz first makes sure that Mazy stays inside the house. Later, he places her in one room. When it's time to leave, he comes close to Mazy. "Fishies!" says Luiz. Mazy loves her crunchy fish treats. Luiz holds out his hand with a few tasty pieces. While Mazy nibbles, he grabs her and holds her close. "There's no escaping now," whispers Luiz. He walks with Mazy to another room and opens the door. Mazy sees the carrier.

SKILL PRACTICE Read the item. Write your response.

1. Why does Luiz trick Mazy?

_____

2. What do both Luiz and Mazy dread? Why?

_____

3. What will Mazy do next? Explain.

_____

_____

STRATEGY PRACTICE Ask a partner questions about the passage that begin with *Why*.

READ THE PASSAGE See if you can tell what Casey may do next.

Casey Can

Casey is nearly 2 years old, and he loves to chatter. His favorite thing to say is, "Me do it!" That's Casey's answer when Mom wants to feed him some peas. That's his response when Dad tries to pour him some milk. And it's what Casey says when Mom wants to wash his face.

With a little help from Dad, Casey pours his own breakfast cereal. He tosses in a handful of berries, too. Then it's time to get dressed. "Me do it!" insists Casey while Mom watches.

Casey pulls on his pants. The zipper is in the back. Then he tugs on his T-shirt. At first, he can't figure out where to put his head. One sleeve sticks straight up. Then, Casey pokes his arm through the other sleeve and smiles with pride. He doesn't know that the T-shirt's tag is on the outside. Casey opens a drawer and pulls out two socks. He plops on the floor and yanks the socks on. One sock is red and one is white. "Me do it!" boasts Casey as he reaches for his shoes.

SKILL PRACTICE Read the item. Write your response.

1. Why does Casey put on his own clothes?

_____

_____

2. What will Casey's parents do once he has finished dressing himself?

_____

_____

3. What will Casey probably do next?

_____

STRATEGY PRACTICE Do you know any small children like Casey? Tell a partner about them.

READ THE PASSAGE   Look for ways hippos are suited to where they live.

Life as a Hippo

Hippos get sunburned easily. Since they live in countries where the sun blazes, their bodies have adapted. Hippos ooze a reddish-colored oil. It covers their skin like a sunscreen.

Hippos also protect their skin by spending most of the day in lakes and rivers. Hippos can stay alert even when their bodies are soaking in water. A hippo's eyes, ears, and nose are on top of its head. A hippo's ears and nose close when it goes underwater. Its eyes can stay open. A thin covering of skin slides over each of the hippo's eyes and work like goggles.

Hippos are huge animals that weigh thousands of pounds. They need to paddle that weight through water. Their feet are webbed like a duck's. Those feet help hippos move their bodies. In shallow water, hippos simply walk with their feet touching the bottom.

These large mammals are plant eaters. Although hippos spend most of the day in water, they do not eat the plants that grow there.

SKILL PRACTICE   Read the item. Write your response.

1. Why did the author write this text?

_____

2. How are a hippo's eyes, ears, and nose specially suited to where it spends its time?

_____

_____

3. What do hippos do after the sun goes down? How do you know?

_____

STRATEGY PRACTICE   Write the question for the part of the passage that you read again.

_____

READ THE AD Read all the parts of this ad.

Puppet-Making Classes

Puppet Power is coming to the **Just for Kids** art center! Join the summertime fun! We'll show you how to create your own great puppet. It's easy to do. We have tons of supplies, so just bring your imagination. Once the puppets are made, you'll decorate the puppet stages. On July 18, invite your family and friends to a puppet show. They'll see what Puppet Power is all about!

What: Puppet Power puppet-making
Where: Just for Kids, 5083 Nile Avenue
When: Saturdays, June 20–July 18
10:00 AM–11:00 AM

Cost: $20.00
Ages: 7–10

Sign up until June 19 at **Just for Kids**.

SKILL PRACTICE Read the item. Write your response.

1. What information is given in the title?

_____

2. Why do you think the ad included a picture?

_____

_____

3. Your little sister is 6. Can she sign up for this puppet-making class? How do you know?

_____

STRATEGY PRACTICE Tell who you think would be most interested in the ad.

_____

READ THE RECIPE Notice how the recipe is organized.

Peanut Butter Cookie Recipe

Ingredients

1 stick of soft butter
½ cup packed brown sugar
½ cup white sugar
½ cup peanut butter
1 egg
1⅓ cups flour
¾ teaspoon baking soda
½ teaspoon baking powder
¼ teaspoon salt

Steps to Follow

1. Use a mixer to stir the butter for 2 minutes until it is creamy. Add the sugars. Mix for 2 more minutes. Mix in the peanut butter and the egg.

2. In a small bowl, mix together the flour, baking soda, baking powder, and salt. Then stir into the butter mixture.

3. Form the dough into a big ball. Wrap it in plastic and refrigerate for 3 hours.

4. Preheat the oven to 375°. Shape dough into small balls. Place them 3 inches apart on an ungreased cookie sheet. Use a fork to make a crisscross pattern on each cookie. Bake for 9 to 10 minutes. Watch to make sure that cookies do not burn. Cool cookies on a rack.

SKILL PRACTICE Read the item. Write your response.

1. Why does the recipe have two parts?

_____

2. You are out of eggs. Should you make the recipe without one or go to the store? Why?

_____

3. Is this recipe one you can make in an hour? How do you know?

_____

_____

STRATEGY PRACTICE Why are the ingredients listed before the cooking instructions?

_____

READ THE INFORMATION   Think about what information the chart gives you.

Who Sleeps the Most?

All animals make time for sleeping. They sleep in different ways. Cows and sheep sleep standing up, and bats sleep upside down. Many birds sleep with their heads tucked under their wings. Different animals sleep different amounts of time. Grazing animals need to eat most of the day. Those animals might spend less time sleeping than other animals do.

Animals	Daily Hours of Sleep
Brown Bat	20
Squirrel	15
Lion	$13\frac{1}{2}$
Cat	12
Dog	$10\frac{1}{2}$
Chimpanzee	$9\frac{1}{2}$
Guppy (fish)	7
Asiatic Elephant	4
Horse	3
Giraffe	2

SKILL PRACTICE   Read the item. Write your response.

1. What is the purpose of the chart?

_____

_____

2. How is the chart organized?

_____

_____

3. How does the text support the chart?

_____

STRATEGY PRACTICE   Underline the sentences in the passage that tell the main idea.

Daily Reading Comprehension • EMC 6363 • © Evan-Moor Corp.

READ THE PASSAGE Use the text and flowchart to understand the information.

Over and Over Again

Most of Earth is covered in water. Earth's water is always moving. It changes from liquid into gas over and over again. This movement of water is called the water cycle. The water cycle has four main actions, shown in the flowchart.

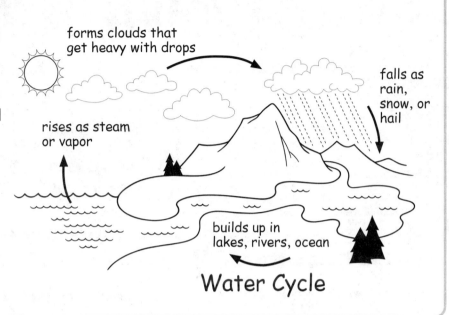

forms clouds that get heavy with drops

falls as rain, snow, or hail

rises as steam or vapor

builds up in lakes, rivers, ocean

Water Cycle

SKILL PRACTICE Read the item. Write your response.

1. What is the purpose of the chart?

_____

_____

2. Look at the chart. What is necessary to make water turn to vapor?

_____

_____

3. Which part of the water cycle could cause a river's banks to overflow? Why?

_____

STRATEGY PRACTICE What other process or cycle could be explained by using a flowchart?

_____

READ THE BULLETIN Notice the different ways the information is presented.

Clown Camp

Today's Zany Fun

- pie-throwing
- juggling
- walking in large shoes
- using a squirting flower
- clown makeup

Snack Bar—Just In!

- yuck-it-up candy bars
- squirt-in-your-face juice
- bubbles-up-your-nose soda

Campfire Tonight

9:00 PM
Outside the **Big Top Tent**

Tales of scary clowns.
Your spine will shiver!
Bring a security blanket
to hold.

Reminders from the Ringmaster

- Write your name inside your wigs and fake noses.
- Keep your clown shoes scuffed and dusty.

Don't Get Lost!

SKILL PRACTICE Read the item. Write your response.

1. How many new items are featured at the snack bar? How do you know?

_____

_____

2. Did clown camp cover riding a unicycle today? How do you know?

_____

3. It's 8:45; you're at the snack bar. You want to go to the campfire. What direction should you go?

_____

STRATEGY PRACTICE Circle the headings in the bulletin. Tell why each is important.

How to Be a Good Reader

Ask yourself these questions to help you understand what you read:

Main Idea and Details	What is the story mostly about? What tells me more about the main idea?
Sequence	What happens first, next, and last? What are the steps to do something?
Cause and Effect	What happens? (the effect) Why did it happen? (the cause)
Fact and Opinion	Can this be proved true? Is it what someone thinks or believes?
Compare and Contrast	How are these people or things the same? How are these people or things different?
Make Inferences	What clues does the story give? What do I know already that will help?
Prediction	What clues does the story give? What do I know already that will help? What will happen next?
Character and Setting	Who or what is the story about? Where and when does the story take place?
Fantasy vs. Reality	Is it make-believe? Could it happen in real life?
Author's Purpose	Does the story entertain, inform, try to persuade me, or teach me how to do something?
Nonfiction Text Features	What kind of text am I reading? What does it tell me?
Visual Information	Is there a picture, chart, or graph? What does it tell me?

Congratulations!

You have
successfully
completed

Daily
Reading
Comprehension

My Notes

My Notes

My Notes

My Notes

My Notes

My Notes